GET MORE PROMISE
OUT OF YOUR LAND

GET MORE PROMISE OUT OF YOUR LAND

by

DON KING

Nicole & Shone
Blessings!

More Promise Publishing, LLC

Edited by: Dan DePriest, Scribe Book Company - Lawton, OK
Cover Design: Susan Browne Designs - Nashville, TN
Cover Photo: (composite image): © 2011 Shutterstock/82143223/Gordon Bell and © 2011 Shutterstock/40112698/Dudarev Mikhail
Interior Design: PerfecType - Nashville, TN

ISBN 978-0-578-09712-1

Printed in the United States by BookMasters Printing - Ashland, OH

Acknowledgments

I have read a thousand books in my life, and I skipped the acknowledgments page when reading the vast majority of those books. Of late, though, I find myself reading books, literally, from cover to cover—including the usually boring acknowledgments page, because now that I know how important these contributions are to projects such as this. Please take a moment to suffer through this page with me.

You may find much in these pages about which to be critical. Pet lovers may hate me and food lovers may think I'm an exercise Nazi. Some will say I ignore 'grace' and I present a 'works-based' gospel. Others will say our salvation is all the 'promise' the Gospel holds forth or that I touch too lightly on faith. If you are someone who has known me, you may even think I'm a hypocrite: "Who is *he* to write a religious book?"

Well, good advice, no matter the source, is good advice. And my fervent prayer is that you find good advice within these pages.

When I gave this message many years ago, my pastor at the time—Farris Whitehead of Eastern Heights Church—said to me, "Son, I really think you have something here . . ." Pastor Farris, whether you meant to or not, that simple bit of encouragement stuck with me and made me want to write this book. I pray, if this book finds its way into your hands, you will be pleased that someone wrote it.

For several years thereafter, I exercised with a wonderful young man—JT Bridges—who fostered a desire in me to write; to go forward with my goals in ministry; and to write *this* book in particular. JT, I miss working out with you and hope your own book endeavors are prospering.

Upon beginning this project, I was encouraged by the congregation and board of directors of RidgeLife Church. Your endorsement of this project and patience with me while I worked on it has been wonderful.

My good friend and fellow laborer in the field, Mr. Jim Gray (among his many contributions), directed me to Mr. Dan DePriest of Scribe Book Company for editing and publishing assistance. I cannot say thank you enough to Dan and his team for all their help getting this book to press. Dan has been so patient and thoughtful while guiding me through this project. This book would have absolutely not been written and published without his help. The perfectionist proofing efforts of Ang DePriest made the manuscript virtually spotless; the cover design by Susan Browne and interior design by Kristin Goble are beyond my best hopes. My endless thanks go to all of you. Now, Jim, we have to get this book out to the world!

Saving the best for last—Mrs. Jeanice King, my beautiful wife and best friend in the world, along with all our wonderful children . . . how blessed am I? Jeanice encouraged me every step of the way to fulfill my life's ambition: to write a book. *Baby, how cool is this!?*

Contents

INTRODUCTION
TWO BOYS FROM TEXAS

If you want to go swimming in the afternoon,
you've got to mow yards in the morning.

I was six years old and my brother Miles was eleven when my family moved to Belton, Texas, shortly after my father was transferred to Fort Hood Army Post in 1959. He was a master sergeant in charge of one of the motor pools for the 1st Cavalry Division stationed there. My mother worked hard as a stay-at-home mom and sometimes as a clerk at Darnell Army Hospital. Neither job paid very well. Our family wasn't exactly poor but we certainly weren't rich either.

Growing up in a small central Texas town during the sixties was unlike anything our children could appreciate today. We learned that life is often about hard decisions. And my mother, thankfully, got those lessons started early on. She was a fastidious housekeeper and did not want us coming in and out of the house messing it up all day; so she kicked us out of the house shortly after breakfast, locked the door, and did not let us back in until just before five o'clock when my father got home for supper. To be fair, I am sure she arranged for lunch, I just don't remember eating any. But, I am serious about her locking the door. So, we couldn't stay home, but we dared not be late for dinner either.

We lived on the outskirts of town—on the last block of the last street in our neighborhood. However, about a mile down the road was . . . Valhalla! Riverside Swimming Pool was like a 1960s version of Wet 'n Wild—a privately owned swimming pool with slides, diving boards, a water wheel, an island in the middle, and a rope with hanging rings we could swing from one at a time and cross the whole length of the pool like Tarzan. It was heaven on a hot Texas summer afternoon.

Miles and I quickly realized that the overall quality of our summer life could be greatly enhanced if we could go swimming at Riverside Pool. There was just one problem: It cost a quarter to get in and our mother was not about to finance such foolishness. She was a frugal and practical woman. So, we faced our first really hard decision; we either found a way to come up with two quarters on our own or we sweltered in the back yard all day.

That decision turned out to be not so hard for us. We decided to borrow our father's lawn mower and go off in search of some kindly person that would let us mow their yard for at least two quarters— not always an easy proposition for an eleven- and six-year-old. But some days we might have made as much as a dollar, which meant not just admission to the pool but a hot dog and an ice cold Coca Cola too. Talk about heaven on earth; cool, clear water on a hot Texas afternoon, pretty girls sunbathing, and a hot dog and soda. Only one way to get there though: if you want to go swimming in the afternoon, you've got to mow yards in the morning.

Lest you think it was easy to accomplish this enterprise on virtually a daily basis, understand that we had to get the lawn mower out of my dad's tool shed. Being a master sergeant in the Army, he kept his tool shed so clean and organized it could have doubled as a hospital operating room. So at the end of each morning's enterprise we had to be sure to return everything to the way it was or we'd hear about it.

Then there was the little problem of gasoline for the mower, which was going for about twelve cents a gallon back then. We had to find a customer, mow their yard, replace the gas, clean the mower, and put it back exactly the way we found it. I have a hard time, in the world we live in, imagining eleven year old boys and their little brothers today pulling that off most every day of their summer.

My parents were tough-minded but fair and loving. No one should think ill of them for raising me to be frugal and independent. They were both Great Depression babies who worked hard all their lives. When he was fifteen, Dad tried to lie about his age to join the Marines at the outbreak of WWII. He succeeded in joining the Navy at sixteen and was soon shipped off to war and saw nine island invasions in the Pacific before he was nineteen. His first three days away from home he spent in the brig on bread and water for being late to his first watch. He admitted to me one day that, alone in that brig, he cried like a baby. But from that time on he became a punctual, no-nonsense man.

A Pattern Develops

One of the amazing things about my youth is how many stories begin with: "Miles got this job, so being the kid brother I had to. . . ." At fourteen, Miles got his driver's license and bought a motorcycle. So he got a newspaper route and together we went into the newspaper delivery business. My mom got us up every morning at 4:00. We met the other newspaper boys on the city square where we had to get the papers, roll them, deliver them, and get back home and off to school by 8:00. Even during the school year, if we wanted to go swimming in the afternoon we had jobs to do first.

A few summers later, Miles got a job working for the county agriculture agency to visit farms around the county and confirm that each field conformed to aerial photographs and was planted according to record. So my job was to run around the perimeter of the fence line to get all the needed information. I ran my legs off that summer, but if I wanted to go swimming in the afternoon . . .

This working relationship with Miles continued into adulthood. Miles eventually married a girl whose father built a nursing home for an investor. When the deal went sour Mile's father-in-law found himself with a nursing home to operate. About that time, the State of Texas enacted new licensure requirements for nursing home administrators, and he decided that nursing homes had a great future, so he insisted that all his children get licensed under the new law—Miles included. Four years later when I graduated from college, Miles helped me get into the business and become an administrator as well.

It's quite a story but the short of it is that over the next three and half decades Miles and I both became very successful in the long-term care industry. Between us we owned or supervised over one hundred long-term care facilities. Together, we have employed several thousand health care workers during our careers, becoming well known in the close-knit world of elder care professionals. We each started several businesses that proved very successful and have enjoyed not just serving people in their time of need but a degree of financial success as well.

Part of my story in these years is becoming a Christian and being led to a church to serve and worship. After years in various lay leadership positions and considerable theological study, including time in the Master's Program at Southwest Assemblies of God University in Waxahachie, Texas, I was ordained by my church to preach the gospel of Jesus Christ. When I sold my last principle business, American Hospice Inc., I thought about retiring or finding some other entrepreneurial pursuit. God, however, had another plan and called me to pastor a small church in southwest Fort Worth. Today, RidgeLife Church is a dynamic and growing congregation and my life is more fun than ever.

About seven years ago, Miles and I, along with our younger sister, got the call that my mother's doctor identified five spots on her lung x-rays. After additional tests she was diagnosed with stage-four bilateral lung cancer and given six months to live. We were devastated and asked her what we could do for her. She answered that she wanted to visit San Francisco. Perhaps the happiest time of my mother's life was when my Dad was in the Navy and they lived in San Francisco. I was born at the Oakland Naval Hospital. So we all took her to visit San Francisco, Napa Valley, and the Monterey Peninsula. It was a great time.

One night, while there, she took Miles and me aside to tell us something confidentially. You must understand that my mother and father had about as dysfunctional a relationship as any two people that love each other can have. Mother never trusted my father's handling of the family's money. I am not sure why, because they both seemed very frugal to me, but that's how it always was. But she had a secret she needed to share with us.

Dad had been in both the Navy and the Army. After retiring from the military, he had several small business ventures that did reasonably well before settling on becoming a barber with a one-man shop. My mother went back to school and became an RN late in life. They did well for themselves after the age of fifty until retiring in their sixties. Dad was first to retire from his barber business due to a worsening service-related disability. A few years later mom also retired. They were not wealthy people by any stretch of the imagination. However, they had saved about $180,000 over the years and fully paid for their three-bedroom, one-bath house, which I grew up in on the outskirts of Belton.

Taking us aside, my mother confided to us that over the years she had saved more than $100,000 without my father's knowledge. It was in a secret bank deposit box in CD's and U.S. Government Bonds already in Miles's, my, and our sister's names.

Miles and I looked at each other. We were incredulous having the same thought at the same time: *All those quarters!!!* All those summer mornings while we were out pushing lawn mowers, she was depositing every quarter she could find into secret bank accounts. We could forgive her, though, because she was thinking of us.

Our mother was a strong woman. She outlived the doctor's expectations, fighting lung cancer for two years. Then, one night in 2004, my father suffered a stroke and died in his sleep. That next morning mother lay down in her bed and followed him seven days later. Literally seven days after he died she died, and her funeral was exactly one week after his.

I was privileged to tell this story at her funeral. Afterward, one of my nieces asked me how they did it. How did these two people of such modest means save nearly $300,000? She went on to tell me that she and her husband both make excellent incomes but had nothing in savings. "What was their secret?" she asked, telling me that they really needed to start a savings program. I told her, "While growing up we never ate out. By that I mean . . . never. I ate a fine steak in a restaurant for the first time in 1976 after I graduated from college and bought it myself." As a boy, I remember a new hamburger place came to town that everyone was talking about where you could get five burgers for a dollar. My mom tried it, but didn't like the burgers and never went back because she could make better burgers at home for less.

"Also while we were growing up we never went on vacation. Again, I mean . . . never! The closest thing to a vacation we ever took was visiting relatives and staying with them. If the road trip required a stop, she packed a lunch so all they had to buy was perhaps a cup of coffee and a drink for us. We didn't go shopping. Mom took us kids to the base PX one time in late summer to buy clothes for the coming school year. She also did all her grocery shopping there. Very rarely would we even buy milk locally.

The more I told my niece, the wider her eyes got. Finally, when I told her no shopping she stopped me and said; "We'll never be able to save if that's what it takes!"

In retrospect I realized that my mother gave me something priceless. My share of the estate is gone but what I learned in Belton, Texas, after the screen door slammed shut and the door lock engaged, built much of my life and sustains me still:

> *If you want to go swimming in the afternoon, you've got*
> *to mow lawns in the morning.*

Thanks, mom!

Hard Decisions

What is it that you want? Do you want a better marriage? Do you want to regain your health, get control of your finances, raise your family in a Christ-centered wholesome manner?

> *If you want to go swimming in the afternoon, you've got*
> *to mow lawns in the morning!*

In a nutshell, that is what this book is about. There are many wonderful promises in the Bible about living well, including promises about your health, your relationships, and even your money. God, however, is not going to take you out and beat you with a blessing stick. And there are no Christianized magic words or short cuts to the Promised Land that God has waiting for you. You have to get off your duff and do some things if you want to get the blessings spoken of in the Bible.

The original title of this book was *Things Are Different West of the Jordan.* The idea was born in me ten years ago when I delivered a message of that title to a men's retreat. It was based on seven powerful principles that Moses shared with the children of Israel while encamped on the east side of the Jordan River and before crossing over into the Promised Land. The address by Moses, recorded in the book of Deuteronomy, includes a promise from God that if the people would cross over the Jordan River and trust Him by obeying Him and the principles given through Moses, the land promised to Abraham would be theirs and they would be abundantly blessed. They would *Get More Promise Out of Their Land.*

But the story in Deuteronomy isn't just for the children of Israel; the Apostle Paul makes that very clear in 1 Corinthians 10:1–6. The Bible reveals that their Promised Land experience was just a first-fruit of God's Kingdom and that we who inherited it by faith are the first-fruits of God's holy people. Israel's history is our lesson book for Kingdom living because God's promises to Israel are also available to us as our inheritance. The Kingdom promises continue and are magnified and fulfilled through Christ, the promised Redeemer. Christ is the ultimate and central fulfillment of all God's promises. And it is Christ's followers who are especially blessed to see God's Kingdom principles come full circle and become clear.

For Moses and Israel, however, God's ordinances were shadowy tests of faith they couldn't fully see or understand. In Christ, we can see the whole picture.

THINGS ARE DIFFERENT
WEST OF THE JORDAN

The land you are entering to take over is not like the land of Egypt, from which you have come, where you planted your seed and irrigated it by foot as in a vegetable garden. But the land you are crossing the Jordan to take possession of is a land of mountains and valleys that drinks rain from heaven.

DEUTERONOMY 11:10

T he Book of Deuteronomy was not my favorite book in the Bible to read. But ten years ago while preparing the message for that men's retreat, I happened to be reading the eleventh chapter of Deuteronomy and the words in verse ten came alive to me, stirring my soul as never before, and a message was born. In a matter of hours I completed notes for my talk at the men's retreat and I'm thankful it was very well received. I began to see that God had given me a message for my life and everyone I could reach, Christian or not, but especially for the Body of Christ.

In Deuteronomy chapter 11, the Israelites are at the end of their forty-year trek through the desert and are preparing to cross the Jordan River and go into the land of Canaan. It is a land, they have been told, flowing with milk and honey. It is a land of promise and plenty for which they have longed for decades.

> Moses tells them how they must live in the Promised Land in order to get the promise out of the Promised Land.

While encamped on the East bank of the Jordan River, Moses holds a kind of spiritual retreat (to put it in modern terms). He calls the people to assemble and, starting with their escape from Egypt and the receipt of the Ten Commandments, he reminds the people of all they have gone through, suffered, and learned over the previous forty years. Most importantly, he tells them how they must live in the Promised Land in order to get the promise out of the Promised Land.

Crossing over Jordan, as a saying, has become analogous to a remarkable change in a person's life or going from a bad situation to a good one. It has, for example, become a metaphor for dying and going to heaven. Likewise, it can refer to a spiritual epiphany. There has even been a TV series, "Crossing Jordan," about a crime-solving spiritualist.

Some Christians compare their salvation experience to crossing the Jordan, meaning they left their old life behind and entered a new life of promise and higher purpose. The analogy, of course, arises out of this biblical account of the Jewish nation escaping the bad situation of bondage in Egypt and entering the Promised Land of Canaan. But to receive the fulfillment of this promise of life change they had to cross over the Jordan River from the east side to the west. Before they did, Moses needed to make clear to them what they were doing was not simply finding a better place to live. They were leaving an old life of slavery and child-like dependence on man and entering a higher life of faith-driven dependence on God and the purposes He had for them.

As we explore the experiences of the Jewish people and the instructions given to them by God for the successful occupation of their Promised Land, we will find universal keys to successful Kingdom living that all persons everywhere can tap into in order to live a more productive and happy life. We will go a step further, however, for there is an even more powerful application of these principals for believers. Believers have been changed by their salvation in Christ. Christ followers have *crossed the Jordan River* and entered their own spiritual Promised Land. Just as it was for the Israelites, it becomes hyper-critical that believers understand these powerful principles of Promised Land living if they are to

> You can't live your new life the old way and expect to see fulfilled any of the promises your new life holds.

13

get more promise out of their land. I am going to say this a lot in the coming pages: You can't live your new life the old way and expect to see fulfilled any of the promises your new life holds.

Birth of a Nation

One of my hopes as you read is that you will gain a sense of connection with ancient Israel and gain some understanding of the context in which Jacob's descendants became the people of God. A messianic Jewish Rabbi friend of mine once remarked about the irony of how Jews have all the symbolic and historical context in their hearts but lack their true Messiah, while Gentile Christians have the true Messiah in their hearts but lack the eye-opening context. In Egypt, the family of Israel grew to a great multitude. Then, at God's appointed time, He led this multitude to the wilderness where He slowly transformed them from a great family with a history to a great people of God with a future. Their future was to cross over Jordan and become a great nation under God.

Many casual readers of the biblical account of Israel's history tend to think of the Israelites' deliverance from slavery in Egypt as a rescue from hardship to the repose of God's provision. I'm afraid that's way off base. If ease and unconcern were what God had in mind for them, they were better off in Egypt. *What?!? In Egypt the Israelites had it EASY? Now, in the Promised Land, they are going to have it HARD?* Well, yes, from a certain point of view that we'll examine more closely in chapter four. The Israelites even complained that life in Egypt was better than the wilderness, even though they were given everything. Moses remembered that and wanted the children of those complainers to understand that the Promised Land was *even farther* from their life in Egypt.

God had been preparing His people to inhabit the Promised Land for generations. God intended to bless all mankind eventually through the Nation of Israel when He would send His Son to redeem all who would call upon His Name. In the meantime, however, God wanted to raise up a People that would recognize Him as the One True God and who would have a unique belief in and reliance upon Him. The children of Israel were the first-fruits of all God's People throughout history from every nation, tongue, tribe, and race who trust Him in that way, including trust in His provision of a Savior.

Humble Beginnings

The history of the descendants of Israel up to that day by the Jordan was one of trial, tribulation, and triumph. It started with Abram, the founding father of their race, urged by the Voice of God to abandon his ancestral home in Ur of the Chaldeans and set upon a nomadic journey. Taking his immediate family and a few relatives and believing he heard from the One True God, he migrates from the fertile valley of the Tigris and Euphrates rivers near Babylonia to the area we now know as Israel.

There, Abram receives a promise from God that one day his descendants will be as numerous as the stars and that the land he is living in (Israel) will belong to them. No longer will they be wanderers, but they will stand as a race of people for the expressed purpose of showing the world that there is a God in Heaven and theirs is the one and only true God. This, in a nutshell, is God's higher purpose for his People in all ages.

Despite the promise to Abram, they get off to a slow start. Abram (now Abraham) has one son in whom the promise is carried forward. Isaac, the child of promise, has two sons—one of whom, Jacob, God re-names *Israel* and declares him the promise-bearer to the next generation. Jacob's twelve sons become the twelve patriarchs of Israel and a race of people is born.

During a time of great famine, Israel takes his whole house of seventy people out of the land in which they have been wandering for three generations. They are called to Egypt by his favorite son, Joseph, whom God has raised to be Prime Minister there. For some time, the descendants or *children* of Israel enjoy great favor and rest from their wanderings. They multiply greatly and, by 400 years passing, become a great nation of people, perhaps as many as a million souls.

However, during those 400 years, a new dynasty of Egyptian pharaohs assume power and enslave the Israelites in order to build its tombs and cities. They are treated so harshly that the Israelites cry out to God for deliverance from their misery. God sees their pain and hears their cries and puts in motion His plan for their deliverance from that old life of drudgery to a life of higher purposes.

After escaping slavery, receiving the Law, and then marching directly to the borders of the Promised Land, the Israelites send in spies to check it out. The spies bring back a single grape cluster so large it had to be carried on a pole between two men. They report the land is good and full of plenty, but that the indigenous population lives in walled cities, are great in strength and number, and giants dwell in the land. Despite the many miracles they experienced up to that point, the children of Israel balk at believing the Lord's assurances that they will successfully take the land.

God then judges that entire generation of former slaves for their unbelief. He forces them to wander in the desert until a new generation, that wouldn't remember Egypt, would stand ready to follow His leading to go in and take the Land for His glory and theirs. Moses dutifully leads the Israelites for the next forty years as he is led by God. During this time of wandering, God miraculously provides food daily in the form of manna. He assures the people of His presence, leading them as a column of smoke by day and a column of fire by night.

Bottom Line

God instructs Moses, who in turn instructs the people how to worship God and how they must live. God meticulously prepares the next generation to follow Him so that they may achieve their destiny. In short, they were as children being provided for and gently raised by their Father God to become strong for Him when, as an adult generation, they would have no fear of obeying Him. Everything God brought Israel through to that time was their prep-school days. At the River Jordan it was time for them to graduate from children of Israel to warriors for God. God is still looking for individuals who will follow Him with child-like faith their whole lives and be strengthened into holy men and women—a people of faith who know the One True God as their Father and declare His Son Jesus Christ as Lord.

New Creatures in Christ

---

*Now, O Israel, listen to the statutes and the judgments which I teach
you to observe, that you may live, and go in and possess the land
which the LORD God of your fathers is giving you."*

MOSES, DEUTERONOMY 4:1; NKJV

*For I want you to know, brothers, that our fathers were all under the
cloud, and all passed through the sea, and all were baptized into
Moses in the cloud and in the sea, and all ate the same spiritual
food, and all drank the same spiritual drink. For they drank from
the spiritual Rock that followed them, and the Rock was Christ.
Nevertheless, with most of them God was not pleased,
for they were overthrown in the wilderness. Now these things took
place as examples for us . . .*

1 CORINTHIANS 10:1–6; ESV

Now these things took place as examples for **us**." The Apostle Paul tells us in his writings to the fledgling Corinthian believers that everything that happened to the Israelites in their desert wanderings and in their Promised Land experiences happened so that we may learn from them. Even 2,000 years later, we can learn from and apply these spiritual truths to our lives. For those of us who aspire to better lives, we can examine the scriptures for spiritual truths and principles that we, too, can implement in order to get more promise out of our land.

The land you are entering to take over is not like the land of Egypt, from which you have come . . . But the land you are crossing the Jordan to take possession of . . . is a land the LORD your God cares for; the eyes of the LORD your God are continually on it from the beginning of the year to its end.

DEUTERONOMY 11:10–12

The connection for the believer is obvious; you are leaving your old life behind and proceeding into a new life. It is even more obvious if we substitute the word *life* for *land*. God is clearly saying to us, "The *life* you are entering into is not like the *life* you had in Egypt. But the *life* you are crossing the Jordan to take possession of is a *life* of mountains and valleys. It is the *life* your God cares for. It is the *life* the eyes of your Lord God are continually on." This is a very sobering and valid truth.

Therefore, if anyone is in Christ, the new creation has come:
The old has gone, the new is here!

2 CORINTHIANS 5:17

The Israelites couldn't have realized the full meaning of what Moses was trying to reveal to them about their new lives any more than the Christian life can be intimately understood until it has been faithfully lived for some time. When the Israelites crossed the Jordan into the Promised Land they experienced a great epiphany.

Imagine with me what it may have been like: The Israelites are encamped on the East Bank of the Jordan River on the morning of their last day before entering the Promised Land. They are encamped as directed by God with the different tribes on both a north/south and east/west axis (forming, literally, a cross) with the Tabernacle of God in the center. A towering pillar of smoke from the very presence of God dominates the landscape rising from the Tabernacle. A million Jews are stirring, naked children run from harried mothers between tents. Young teens are sent out to gather that morning's manna. Later, they all are eating a porridge made from that day's collection. Someone complains, "Manna again," and a wise grandmother retorts, "Someday soon you'll be wishing we had manna!"

After forty years of this routine they must have accepted it as 'normal'—as though this was how things would always be. But, of course, it wasn't normal. The Bible tells us in Deuteronomy 29:5 that God miraculously cared for them during their wanderings, even to the place that neither their clothes nor their shoes wore out.

Soon the shofar blasts and the priests take a step toward the Jordan River with the Ark of the Covenant aloft on their shoulders. What incredible faith they displayed as they walked toward a river swollen with flood water. Yet, as the first priest's foot touches the water, it begins to stop flowing and indeed back up. Soon it stands as a heap of water and backs all the way up to a town called Adam. The ground then supernaturally dries up for them to cross over.

The people begin to pass over and when the first Israelite touches the far shore a curious thing happens: A microscopic sliver of shoe leather flakes off of his sandal for the first time in forty years. Later, someone snags his tunic resulting in a tear, and he doesn't understand what just happened. After all cross over and the Ark is brought over, the river returns to its normal flow and the column of smoke dissipates. That night, they sit in the dark with no column of fire and eat the last manna anyone will ever see. Tomorrow they have to find their own food and take care of themselves . . . in the Promised Land.

Their lives were radically changed, and in time they began to understand. Likewise, when you accept Christ as your Savior you experience not just a great epiphany; there is a radical change in your being. If you experienced the touch of Christ in your life you know exactly what I mean. If you have not, please keep reading. You are in for an interesting and perhaps life changing experience. Let's take a closer look at what Paul means in 2 Corinthians 5:17 when he says we are *new* creatures. The following comes from a widely used and accepted Bible commentary:

"New" in the Greek implies a new nature quite different from anything previously existing, not merely recent, which is expressed by a different Greek word (found in Galatians 6:15). "Creature" means literally, "creation," and so [one becomes] the creature resulting from the creation [of a new being].

JAMIESON, FAUSSET, BROWN COMMENTARY

I want to put forth a bold proposition. First, the Kingdom principles we will be discussing in the following chapters can apply, if practiced, for the betterment of any person's life. However, God's spiritual Laws and Principles apply to the Christian's new nature in a more powerful and personal way. Christians (that is, those who accept Jesus Christ as Lord and Savior and the salvation He bought for them) literally become new persons, whether they feel like it yet or not; whether they look like it yet or not. Their new paradigm, according to Paul, is that they will have been changed, radically and completely, after accepting Jesus as Lord. (Romans 8:29–30, 12:2). Therefore, this temporal life will either be more blessed or more frustrated depending upon his adherence to these Laws and Principles. That's the other side of why living in the Promised Land is full of hard choices. God was very clear to the Israelites: *You live there My way*

> God's spiritual Laws and Principles apply to the Christian's new nature in a more powerful and personal way.

and you will be blessed! Live there your old way, or just any way you want, and not only will you not be blessed but you will be cursed! That shouldn't represent a *hard* decision but we all know that doing the right thing is not always our first impulse even as born-again believers in the Lord Jesus Christ.

Let's unpack this a bit more. Everything else in this book is rooted in this central Truth. Nothing else is as foundational to understanding the miracle and genius of God's plan of salvation for you and me. When a person accepts Christ for the redemption He purchased for us on the Cross, an actual, not just figurative, change takes place in him. His dead spirit is made alive through the power of Christ's own resurrection. That is the part God sees clearly as a new man with no history of sin. The new Christian's soul, as well, begins to transform from the dying mind-emotions-and-will it was before, into a soul that is empowered to turn about, change directions, and begin healing and growing powerful in Christ's strength. Both a creative event and a re-creative process occur that leave him a different person from the inside out. He has a fresh beginning. The grace of God has regenerated him. A Christian, quite literally, becomes a new creature.

> When a person accepts Christ, an actual, not just figurative, change takes place in him.

Regenerating grace creates a new world in the soul; all things are new. The renewed man acts from new principles, by new rules, with new ends, and in new company.

MATTHEW HENRY COMMENTARY

"Regenerating grace creates a new world in the soul . . ." I wish I had the time and space to tackle "grace" and "soul" in this work. For now, we can simply understand that God creates a change within us that brings us both special opportunities and special responsibilities. We are mysteriously and marvelously made into a new man. This change is greater than a mere spiritual epiphany. This is a profound change from a degenerate being to one who is *restored to life* and enabled to have a relationship with his Creator that he couldn't have before.

"The renewed man acts from new principles, by new rules, with new ends, and in new company." I urge every member of my congregation to write those words, as I have done, on the inside cover of their Bibles. For all who seek a better life, there are few sentences in the English language more concisely meaningful and instructive. Let's break it down in detail:

"The renewed man acts . . ." Our base nature is so overwhelmed by this regenerating change that we forever forsake our old sinful ways and embark on a new enlightened existence free from sin and live in idyllic communion with the Creator. Not so. Much like the sobering caution Moses gave the Israelites, you, too, may find you had it easier in Egypt (your old life) than you do in this Promised Land (your new life). Every believer learns we must undertake a substantial degree of discipline to "act" or live out our faith and the truths of our Lord.

". . . from new principles, by new rules, with new ends . . ." What did Moses tell the Israelites?

The LORD will establish you as a holy people to Himself,
just as He has sworn to you, if you keep the commandments of the
LORD your God and walk in His ways. Then all peoples of the earth
shall see that you are called by the name of the LORD,
and they shall be afraid of you. And the LORD will grant you plenty
of goods, in the fruit of your body, in the increase of your livestock,
and in the produce of your ground, in the land of which the
LORD swore to your fathers to give you.

DEUTERONOMY 28:910; NKJV

> This new life in Christ is a *new* life, one that the Lord cares about with ample provision.

A new life, with new rules . . . yes, but with new and better ends! The life you are entering into, when you are called by His Name as a Christian, is not like the old life you used to live in. This new life in Christ is a *new* life, one that the Lord cares about with ample provision. It is a life He has His eyes on. It is a life that holds great calling and a great deal of promise. It is a renewed life with new ends, new outcomes, and better promises. It is a life in which you can access or obtain the promise if you live it according to certain principles.

"**. . . and in new company.**" The Promised Land promises involve universal rules and principles. They apply to all God's human creation. They do not work just for believers. They work for all men everywhere. But (and this is important!), they work better and more powerfully for the renewed man with his changed nature.

Bottom Line

With the creation of the Universe and its physical laws, God put in motion Laws and Principles that govern our lives and fruitfulness. Just as the law of gravity applies to believer and non-believer alike, His Spiritual Laws and Principles apply to believer and non-believer alike. The Principle of giving yields a return for the atheistic philanthropist as it does the church tither. But, again, it works better, more predictably, and, most importantly, with God's favor upon us believers due to our changed nature.

This, I believe, explains the frustration many Christians often experience. So often we try to continue to live our new lives the old way, either through ignorance, disbelief, or lack of faith. It just doesn't work and hopefully one learns this sooner rather than later. So often, however, we see the ardor of love for the Lord fade as the new Christian faces adversity, trials, and tribulation.

The Christian can still live out the sin and self-destructive behavior of the old life, it just won't be so much fun anymore. Why? Because the Christian has been changed! From the inside out, a miraculous change has taken place. The old lusts, vengefulness, and selfishness now leave a sour taste in the mouth. The stain of sin is more visible, its stench more pungent to us, its shame more debilitating. Now, unless you determine to live this new life the way God instructs, you'll become disappointed and disheartened; always frustrated because you are a new man trying to live the old way.

Jesus Himself said, *"No one puts a piece of unshrunk cloth on an old garment; for the patch pulls away from the garment, and the tear is made worse. Nor do they put new wine into old wineskins, or else the wineskins break, the wine is spilled, and the wineskins are ruined. But they put new wine into new wineskins, and both are preserved"* (Matthew 9:16–17; NKJV). Jesus teaches that the Christian experiences newness in his life that is completely incompatible with his old life.

We have all experienced the frustration and anguish of temptation and failure. Some personal demon seeks to drag us back into sin we used to indulge in. If we fail, that lust is satisfied for the moment; but then our new nature is so offended the remorse we feel is staggering. I have personally dealt with this and have lost track of how many other believers I've sought to console and encourage through this experience. Again, the central Truth is key to our victory. The sooner we realize we are new creatures and that we will never again be anything other than new creatures, the sooner we can rid ourselves of those sin habits. We can finally bring to the surface of our lives and fully experience another Truth that is already true of us:

> *. . . Don't you know that all of us who were baptized into Christ Jesus were baptized into his death? We were therefore buried with him through baptism into death in order that, just as Christ was raised from the dead through the glory of the Father, we too may live a new life.*

> ROMANS 6:3–4

BONDAGE, TRANSITION, TRANSFORMATION

---

*For the LORD your God is bringing you into a good land, a land
of brooks of water, of fountains and springs, that flow out of valleys
and hills; a land of wheat and barley, of vines and fig trees and
pomegranates, a land of olive oil and honey; a land in which you will
eat bread without scarcity, in which you will lack nothing; a land
whose stones are iron and out of whose hills you can dig copper.*

DEUTERONOMY 8:7-9; NKJV

Have you ever thought, with all the promises in the Bible,
*My Christian walk just shouldn't be this hard. Why? Why,
is it so hard?* Have you ever said to a friend, "I love God, I have
accepted Jesus as my Lord, I pray, and yet I don't seem to be getting
anywhere"?

We go through life, we stumble around in the darkness, we find this light—this marvelous Light—and we accept Jesus. We cross the Jordan and find this place called the Promised Land. We have the Bible, we have prayer, we have an evolving understanding of who our God is—that he is our Father, our Abba Father—and yet life is still so hard.

Let me give you three Truths you must not forget:

1. Jesus Christ Almighty declared, "I have come that they may have life, and have it to the full" (John 10:10). Jesus came so that *you* would experience this . . . *you*, not just some lucky few. But . . .

2. There is a thief too. If you believe in God you have to understand there is a thief and his name is Satan, or *Ha'Satan'* in the Hebrew text. The Bible says that he comes to steal from you, to destroy you, and to kill you (John 10:10; 1 Peter 5:8). Therefore, it is critical that we know how to live in this new life in order to void the efforts of our enemy and enjoy the benefits of this new life. Make sense?

3. Satan's evil works, however, are not to be convenient excuses for bad things our own choices bring. Sadly, if we are ignorant of how to live in the Promised Land or too willful to change, we can actually still live in a cursed condition despite being born again (Deuteronomy 28:15–20).

As we examine scripture and look for analogies to our Christian walk in the Israelites' experience, we may see that we have an upside-down view of what we should expect as we move from a place of bondage (Egypt), through a period of transition (the desert), to transformation (the Promised Land). We may discover that our expectations for each period are erroneous and questions about our experiences in each stage may be answered.

The Proving Ground

Several times the wandering Israelites complained bitterly about how much better they had it back in Egypt when confronted with the difficulties of their desert experience: "the Israelites started wailing and said, "If only we had meat to eat! We remember the fish we ate in Egypt at no cost—also the cucumbers, melons, leeks, onions and garlic" (Numbers 11:4–5).

Further, while in the desert they experienced many miracles—so many that we might easily confuse their desert experience as what we should expect of *our* Promised Land experiences. Examples: God led them visibly by day as a column of smoke and at night as a column of fire. God fed them miraculously every day and on special occasions. God spoke to their leader face-to-face as man might to another man. Aaron's rod budded. The Bible says that, during the entire desert wanderings, neither their clothes nor their shoes wore out. Now that is what I would call some good Promised Land miracles! Except they didn't happen in the Promised Land but in the desert.

In the Promised Land, their shoes began to wear out and their clothes grew old. In the Promised Land, they had to find their own food every day, for the first time in their lives! In the Promised Land, they had to work for everything they needed and wanted.

> In the Promised Land, they had to work for everything they needed and wanted.

Did I say *work?* Excuse me. In the Promised Land, they had to *fight* for everything they wanted and needed . . . they had to fight giants . . . they had to fight giants who lived in walled cities. Moses told them the Promised Land was everything good that they expected it to be. But they had to live in it God's way and not their own way if they expected to realize the promise that the Promised Land held for them.

After forty years of wandering in the wilderness, a new generation of Israelites, still led by Moses, finds itself on the East Bank of the Jordan River, presumably ready to cross over and take the Promised Land. It is a moment for which they have prepared all their lives. They have come to enter the Promised Land—the land that flows with milk and honey, where they will cease their wandering and become a great nation. It is the land promised to their forefathers.

Like a fretting grandfather, Moses reminds them of how they must go in and *take* the land, and he gives his last address to them as to how they must live there. Over and over, he tells them that to get the *promise* out of the land of Promise they have to live a certain way—God's way and not their own. He tells them, in fact, that things are going to be very different west of the Jordan, and that he will not be going over with them; instead they will be led by his protégé, Joshua.

Here is the hard part about why their fathers and especially they (up until then) had it easier than they will in the Promised Land— the hard decision: From that day on they must witness God through the eyes of faith. For no longer will God carry them as a man carries his son; as He did in all the way, that they went until they came to this place. (Deuteronomy 1:31) God went in the way before them to search out a place for them to pitch their tents; to show them the way they should go, in the fire by night and in the cloud by day. (Deuteronomy 1:33) All of those "childhood" provisions will cease the moment they receive and act on God's promise by crossing over the Jordan.

While in Egypt, the children of Israel were in bondage but they were not without a minimum of provision. "Up to this point you've had it as easy as children," paraphrasing Moses, "even as slaves in Egypt" (Deuteronomy 11:10–11). "All you had to do was scrape your big toe in the rich, muddy shores of the Nile River, throw out some seeds and up would sprout a vegetable garden." They didn't have to defend against Egypt's enemies or consider how they would be fed. They had adequate housing, abundant water; and Goshen, their district, was actually the most fertile part of Egypt. But their labor was not spent to provide for themselves and enlarge their own potential. Their labor and productivity was forced to strengthen first the Egyptians. They weren't able to choose the risks and possibilities that come with freedom.

> It will take hard work, daring, and diligent adherence to God's principles to get the *promise* out of the Promised Land.

Before crossing the Jordan, Moses tells the people that the Promised Land is not going to be like that. It has hills and valleys (ups and downs) and it drinks the rain of heaven (perspiration) from hard work to make it productive. Moses tells them it will take hard work, daring, and diligent adherence to God's principles to get the *promise* out of the Promised Land. But the land will be theirs, they will be free, and they will be the people of the One True God.

The Believer's Journey

Because the experiences of Israel are an example to us (1 Corinthians 10:6), we can see Egypt, where the Israelites were held as slaves, as a metaphor for *bondage*, or *the world system of unregenerate man*, and also as our life before Christ when we were in the world and in bondage to it. The Egyptians worshipped the creation rather than the Creator. They worshipped all manner of animals, birds, reptiles, and even the Nile River. Thus it is a perfect metaphor for the world, and secular humanism in particular, because of the center place of man and his works in those systems. In Egypt, the Israelites lived in the most fertile district of the Nile delta but were put to bondage, harsh treatment, and cruelty. This is a perfect metaphor for the mixed, bitter-sweet experience of bondage to sin and the world's values. Its indulgences and self-justifications are often sweet on the tongue but always sour in the belly. No matter how free and independent one may feel, without the kind of freedom Christ offers, the truth is, people get used to living in bondage and even cling to its familiarity. We all feel the pressure of this truth when we sense the calling to escape because the uncertainties and risks of freedom are more frightening than the bondages we've adapted to.

The Desert is a metaphor for a time of transition. God took the children of Israel out of bondage and transitioned them to the Promised Land. Slowly, they transitioned from a nation of former slaves to a free and independent people. They were free of the harsh life of bondage but they had many trials as they wandered in the wilderness. Their difficulties and dangers helped them grow and mature into a strong nation. This wilderness transition is exactly what the metaphor points to for us as sojourning former slaves and now followers

> *The Promised Land* is a metaphor for fundamental transformation

of Christ growing and maturing into a strong and holy nation (1 Peter 2:9). When we accept Christ we are relieved of our bondage and begin transitioning to a new life in Christ.

The Promised Land is a metaphor for fundamental transformation—something totally new and unknown. In the Promised Land, the children of Israel assumed their role as a sovereign nation under God. Here they saw fulfillment of all the promises made to them by

God over hundreds of years. Moses, in Deuteronomy 8, provides a glorious description of the rich blessings to be had in the Promised Land:

For the LORD your God is bringing you into a good land—a land with streams and pools of water, with springs flowing in the valleys and hills; a land with wheat and barley, vines and fig trees, pomegranates, olive oil and honey; a land where bread will not be scarce and you will lack nothing; a land where the rocks are iron and you can dig copper out of the hills.

DEUTERONOMY 8:7–9

What a wonderful metaphor for a new life! All those obvious blessings translate to a better life today for you, the Believer! So, wouldn't it seem logical to presume from these metaphors that each stage of life should be easier than the next? We can easily understand that Egypt means bondage for us. When you are in the world, in bondage, you have it tough. And we understand that in the desert we are in transition from babes in the faith to responsible people of God. So all the stumbling difficulties of transition should ultimately be worth it as you finally transform to Promised Land living, right? And then you live a life in which you enjoy all the wonderful promises of rest given in the Bible for the believer.

However, the wisdom to see the hidden truth in these metaphors, which tend to contradict our simpler, natural presumptions, is part of what we gain in our Promised Land transformation.

A New Kind of Rest

Egypt

Egypt, as a metaphor, represents the world and unregenerate life. Millions of people live unregenerate lives in the world and think they are perfectly fine and normal. Hurt, pain, disappointment, even bondage to sin are all part of "normal" life. There even exists a perverted sense of freedom from what are erroneously perceived as *the unfair and narrow-minded restrictions of organized religion on personal choices and human expression*. But to understand Egypt is to know it as a place of bondage. That's hard to do if you've never known anything else. How does a person blind from birth ever truly understand what he is missing and value it as much as one who lost his sight in the prime of his life? By the same token, the children of Israel could never have understood or wisely lived with the preciousness and power of freedom until they had learned, over a long period, that real freedom is preserved and made fruitful through trust in God.

But the Promised Land isn't primarily a metaphor for a new life of freedom. A *free* life, of course, was one of the fruits of crossing the Jordan and taking the Land. The real

> The Promised Land is about a *changed* life.

metaphor is about a *changed* life—a life lived with new motivations and perspectives. A Promised Land life is continually re-created, energized, and glorified by the fulfillment of God's promises. And chief among these is the promised Redeemer and the rest He brings.

So, a certain kind of rest is what this metaphor of transformation involves. It is not a rest of ease and leisure. It is a rest from the fear of man and the fear of failure. The Promised Land is a good land, rich with the raw provisions that a productive, holy life need only dig up and use faithfully (Deuteronomy 8:7–9). God promised fruitfulness to the faithful of His people. In fact, He promised that everything they do will profit them (Deuteronomy 29:9, 1 Chronicles 22:12–13, Psalm 1:1–3). What better promise, what greater freedom, could we desire than to know we can't fail if we don't give up or give in to destructive temptations?

But even in our sins we have direct access to our Redeemer who forgives and restores. That's what Israel had to look forward to in the Promised Land. Their labors and battles to claim the Land were promised to be fruitful for their own sakes and their descendants. But it involved a two-sided covenant as the above-noted scripture portions make clear. The promises were contingent on their having pure hearts before God—hearts unstained by rebellion to His statutes and principles.

The Wilderness

If we cry out to the One True God; God Almighty, Creator of the Universe, and accept His Son Jesus Christ as our savior, we experience a miracle, we are born again. We begin a journey of transition. Through the washing of the Word and the renewing of our spirits we become new persons. It truly is a miraculous process. The process can be an unbroken and powerful life-changing direction of growth in Christ's strength. It can also be a continual pattern of wandering in the desert of willful self-gratification, often referred to as *backsliding*, to seasons of restoring repentance and back again. Israel wandered needlessly in the desert for forty years because they looked to their own fearfully meager strength instead of God's proven trustworthiness to change their lives. Being stuck in the Desert is no more fun for you today than it was for the children of Israel. You

> You have to enter into The Promised Land and do some things to appropriate all its blessings.

don't have to be. You can begin right where you are, walk right up to the Promised Land and enter in right now. Understand this: Upon accepting Jesus as Lord you are saved. You are born again. Your salvation is sure. But God's miracle life is not automatic. You have to enter into the Promised Land and do some things to appropriate all its blessings.

The Promised Land

The Promised Land is the stage of life God wants you living in. He wants all believers living lives of faith, grounded in His principles to successfully occupy the Promised Land. Yes, it is a land of hills and valleys (ups and downs). Yes, it drinks the rain of heaven (it takes effort to make it work). It is inhabited by giants (challenges) and walled cities (obstacles). Your shoes, your clothes, and even your bodies will wear out even though you fight the good fight of faith. But these costs, if they can be called that, are nothing compared to the glory of the promises.

Blessed will you be in the city and in the country. Your children will be blessed. God will command a blessing upon all that you do— your work, your home, and your lives. The Lord will command your enemies to flee from you. God will establish you among His holy people. He will cause you to have plenty. God will open to you His treasure. People will call you blessed. God will make you the head and not the tail, above and not beneath.

DEUTERONOMY 28:1–13; PARAPHRASED

. . . there need be no poor people among you, for in the land the LORD your God is giving you to possess as your inheritance, he will richly bless you, if only you fully obey the LORD your God and are careful to follow all these commands I am giving you today. For the LORD your God will bless you as he has promised, and you will lend to many nations but will borrow from none. You will rule over many nations but none will rule over you.

DEUTERONOMY 15:4–6

Bottom Line

So the metaphors are correct but we have to look at them correctly to appreciate them. Egypt does indeed represent the world's system and values and our natural born bondage to them. Our lives begin innocently enough but as we grow older we all face some kind of bondage in the world. Sin, addiction, bad relationships, failed marriages, and personal failings take their toll. We develop character flaws and bad habits from years of practicing the world's way of seeking personal comfort and avoiding pain. It often takes us a long time to recognize that the cycles of addiction to the world lead to self-destruction. It's only through God's mercy that we may come to the place where we cry out to Him, "There has to be something better than this!"

This is the promise to be experienced in the Promised Land to where you have been called. But, again, fulfillment of the above promise is a two-way covenant. Your side of the covenant is to live in the Promised Land God's way and not your way. There are seven principles for successful Promised Land living given by Moses to the Children of Israel that apply to us today. We begin in the next chapter with the first and foremost principle.

PRINCIPLE #1
LOVE THE LORD YOUR GOD

Keep the Main Thing the Main Thing!

Hear, O Israel: The LORD our God, the LORD is one. Love the LORD your God with all your heart and with all your soul and with all your strength.

DEUTERONOMY 6:4–5

Jesus said to him, " 'You shall love the LORD your God with all your heart, with all your soul, and with all your mind.' This is the first and great commandment. And the second is like it: 'You shall love your neighbor as yourself.' On these two commandments hang all the Law and the Prophets."

MATTHEW 22:37–40; NKJV

Love the LORD your God. This is the first Principle you must embrace in order to get more promise out of your land. It is the bedrock truth upon which all other truth is built and upon which our lives must be built. The LORD our God is one. Our best words fail to capture the depth of that phrase but suffice it for this lesson to understand that the LORD God alone is self-existent and self-significant. All other beings and all other things in space, matter, time, or eternity exist by and for the LORD. The true and central significance of all that exists is in the LORD God Himself. That is why the words of Deuteronomy 6:4–5 were central to the morning, day, and evening prayers of Israel (known in Hebrew as the *Sh'ma*) in obedience to God's command in verse 7. We are to look upon the LORD God as our centrality and significance when we rise up, when we lie down, and when we walk in the way. When we do, a desire for intimacy with Him grows as indicated by the call in verse 5 to "Love the LORD your God, with all your heart, all your soul and all your strength."

Both Moses and Jesus taught this as the fundamental principle upon which to build your life. It is the true meaning of life and the beginning and end of everything that matters. There is a God—He is the God of Holy Scripture and Jesus Christ is His Son. He chose to reveal Himself more completely to us through His Holy Word, the Bible, and our unarguable response to this Truth is to marvel at and revere Him.

God *is* God and there is no other. He is the Holy One of Israel. His is the Name the early Jews would not utter for reverence of Him. God is a person, not an impersonal force. In short, God is a *Who* not a *what*. And we can see a glimpse of Who God is in the descriptive names for Him we find in the Bible. Among those names are Provider, Healer, Shepherd, Sanctifier, Banner, Peace, and Lord of Hosts.

Jesus is His only Son. Jesus was with God at the creation of the Universe as the second person in the Trinity. At the appointed time, He stepped out of eternity and into a cradle. He was born a man, He suffered as we suffer, felt pain we feel, endured temptation as we endure it. He, however, was able to do so successfully, and thus led a completely sin-free life and was, therefore, an acceptable sacrifice for all mankind. To be saved, one has to accept and believe that Jesus died for him or her personally. We must repent of our sins and accept Him as Lord and Savior. In time, our understanding of the complexities of the Faith we have accepted may improve, but simple child-like faith in the Lordship of Jesus Christ is all we need to begin that journey. He is the Lamb of God, the Christ, the Messiah, the Lion of Judah, Prince of Peace, Lord of lords, and God of gods. It is He to whom every knee shall bow and every tongue shall confess is Lord. He is the Way, the Truth, and the Life. The only way to God is through Him and a saving knowledge of who He is (Isaiah 9:6; John 1:36, 14:6; Philippians 2:10–11; Revelation 5:5).

God, the God of the Bible, is the Creator of Heaven and earth. As such, He is worthy of our love and devotion. We are admonished to do so at least fifteen times in the book of Deuteronomy alone. Most of these verses contain various promises—that in return for our devotion:

He will make you prosperous in all the work of your hands (24:19, 28:12).
He will bless your crops and herds (what you do for a living) (7:13, 28:4).

He will send rain to bless the harvest (make your work fruit-ful) (16:15).

He will bless you with strength to take the Land and live in it (11:8).

He will keep His covenant of love for a thousand genera-tions to those that love Him (5:10, 7:9).

He will increase your numbers (7:13).

He will bless the fruit of your womb (your children) (7:13, 28:4).

He will keep you free from disease (7:15).

Certainly these promises are thrilling in and of themselves, but God deserves our love with or without a promise. Knowing such a God exists is enough to inspire worship of Him. Yet there they are, promise after promise after promise. The reason has to be that God loves and thrills to bless us just as we do our own children. And yet we most desire to see our children become strong, principled, noble men and women of God. So if we are wise, we are careful not to spoil them by giving in to our impulse to lavish them with unearned blessings. We teach them that our desire is to richly bless them and to give them well-defined paths to that blessing as they grow. And the first path must be that they never forget to honor their father and mother. This should make it very easy to understand the heart of God. Our gentlest and most noble instincts are like God's because we are made in His image. So, because God is our true Father, it is clear that to appropriate the Promise out of the Promised Land one must *Love the LORD your God.*

Okay, How Do We Do That?

God has mandated that He comes first above ALL things. True love is about putting the object of your love first and above competing interests, much like a husband should show his wife, forsaking all other would be-lovers. God went to great lengths to instruct Israel through Moses how to ensure that they and future generations would always put Him first. It is again found in Deuteronomy:

> God, has mandated that He comes first above ALL things.

When the LORD your God brings you into the land you are entering to possess and drives out before you many nations—the Hittites, Girgashites, Amorites, Canaanites, Perizzites, Hivites and Jebusites, seven nations larger and stronger than you—and when the LORD your God has delivered them over to you and you have defeated them, then you must destroy them totally. Make no treaty with them, and show them no mercy. Do not intermarry with them. Do not give your daughters to their sons or take their daughters for your sons, for they will turn your children away from following me to serve other gods, and the LORD's anger will burn against you and will quickly destroy you. This is what you are to do to them: Break down their altars, smash their sacred stones, cut down their Asherah poles and burn their idols in the fire. For you are a people holy to the LORD your God. The LORD your God has chosen you out of all the peoples on the face of the earth to be his people, his treasured possession.

DEUTERONOMY 7:1–6

Remember! This is a metaphor for us today and it's a powerful one. If you have confessed Jesus Christ as your Lord and Savior, you have had a spiritual epiphany and crossed over the Jordan into the Promised Land. What fellowship now can your new light have with darkness (2 Corinthians 6:14)? You must turn from your old habits of personal destruction in order to truly put God first place in your life.

> You must turn from your old habits of personal destruction in order to truly put God first place in your life.

Let's frame this in language we can understand. Most of us find the Lord because we are frustrated with bad habits, bad relationships, bondage to sin, etc. If you continue to have a bad habit or other personal issue that distracts you from a growing and productive relationship with God after coming to Him, then you have to *destroy* the power of that thing, habit, secret sin, or self-interest. Break it down and smash it. Listen to the advice of Moses; don't make a treaty with it; don't show it any mercy; don't associate with it. Kill it! Kill it in your generation so it won't pass on to your sons and daughters as a generational sin or become a root of bitterness in them.

There may be people or places that you associate with that are a problem. The remedy to break the curse of that thing in your life may seem a bit drastic, but don't go there anymore. Don't hang out with those people. Don't keep souvenirs of your problem. Don't try to cut back on your problem. Turn your back on that problem and face the Lord. "Have nothing to do with the fruitless deeds of darkness. . . ." (Ephesians 5:11). Show that you love the Lord your God completely, by completely turning from those old ways and habits. That's how you put Him first place in your life.

After more than twenty years, there are places and parts of town that still remind me of my old life and my old ways. I don't like to be in those areas. I can't tell you how many people tell me that when they are in the company of certain people their salvation goes out the window and they slip back into old discarded habits and ways. Kill it; starve it to death. Break that habit and find new friends or move if you have to.

If you try to occupy the Promised Land while doing the same old things in the same old ways you will not achieve new results. I can guarantee that not only will you not see the fruit of the land but you will be frustrated and miserable as well. This is not just a biblical principle but a practical one as well.

Over and over, I talk with people who are hurt and confused in their walk with the Lord. They read the promises; they see other people enjoying the fruit of the land. Yet they themselves remain in bondage. Having found the Lord, they are more frustrated than before. The life they yearn for seems just out of reach. Yet they cling to old habits and ways. Don't be like them, but learn from their error. Destroy the old ways totally and put God first place in your life.

So if you faithfully obey the commands I am giving you today—to love the LORD your God and to serve him with all your heart and with all your soul—then I will send rain on your land in its season,

*both autumn and spring rains, so that you may gather in your grain,
new wine and oil. I will provide grass in the fields for your cattle,
and you will eat and be satisfied. Be careful, or you will be enticed to
turn away and worship other gods and bow down to them. Then the
LORD's anger will burn against you, and he will shut the heavens so
that it will not rain and the ground will yield no produce, and you will
soon perish from the good land the LORD is giving you.*

DEUTERONOMY 11:13–17

I do not know how our Lord could be clearer: Faithfully obey
His command to put Him first in your life above all other things and
you will be blessed. Allow yourself to be turned away to idolatrous
things and God will discipline you like a faithful Father. What did
Jesus say?

*I will show you what he is like who comes to me and hears my
words and puts them into practice. He is like a man building
a house, who dug down deep and laid the foundation on rock.
When the flood came, the torrent struck that house but could not
shake it, because it was well built. The man who did not was
washed away by his problems.*

(Luke 6:46–49; paraphrased)

The firm foundation of your life in the Promised Land must be
your right relationship with God. It is confessing Jesus Christ as
your Lord and Savior. It is being fixed and firm; unshakable in your

faith and trust in God. It is loving the Lord your God with all your heart, all your mind, and all your might.

Moses went on to give the Israelites more valuable teaching on how to put God first in their lives. And Jewish people to this day place *mezuzahs* on their door posts with an inscription, or *klaf*, tucked inside after being carefully prepared in connection with a blood sacrifice (usually a sheep). The inscription records twenty-two lines of promise from Deuteronomy, chapters 6 and 11. It begins with "Hear, O Israel, the L-rd is our G-d, the L-rd is one. You shall love the L-rd, your G-d, with all your heart, with all your soul, and with all your resources." The portion below from Deuteronomy 11 is also part of the *mezuzah* text.[1]

Teach—Talk—Write

Fix these words of mine in your hearts and minds; tie them as symbols on your hands and bind them on your foreheads. Teach them to your children, talking about them when you sit at home and when you walk along the road, when you lie down and when you get up. Write them on the door frames of your houses and on your gates, so that your days and the days of your children may be many in the land that the LORD swore to give your ancestors, as many as the days that the heavens are above the earth.

Deuteronomy 11:18–21

Let the message of Christ dwell among you richly as you teach and admonish one another with all wisdom through psalms, hymns, and songs from the Spirit, singing to God with gratitude in your hearts.

COLOSSIANS 3:16

God knows that putting Him first, even in the Promised Land, is not easy. It sounds simple but it's quite hard at times, as anyone knows who has struggled a while to live by faith in God's promises. With all the distractions life in the world has to offer, it is very easy to drift and stop putting God first.

Every believer has experienced this, because none of us are perfect. As I talk with people, they are often disheartened that they are so easily distracted by remnants of their old life as well as the influx of new influences. They are discouraged by sin and the lack of spiritual fruit in their lives.

Remember that in Christ we have been fundamentally changed. Doesn't it make sense that the *new man* in each of us will be offended by the *old ways*? Through transformation in Christ, the conscience is cleansed. Now when we fall into sin or old habits it still may gratify for a while, but our new living spirits and consciences will be sickened. We will feel the sting of conviction that these old things are harmful to our walk with God and to our potential in the Promised Land. I have told my church: Once you accept the Lord, you are never going to be the same sinner again. You can try but it just won't be the same anymore. As destructive as the old ways were in Egypt, in the Promised Land everything is amplified. The power of faith in those who know Christ yields far greater growth and glory than ever before possible. On the other hand, all things, circumstances, and consequences in the Promised Land also work much more instantly and effectively to train God's people to trust and follow Him faithfully. God is the perfect Father to us all. He won't crush our spirits with burdens or discipline too great for us to bear. But He doesn't want us spending long decaying lives being fruitless and self-destructive either. God our Father strives with us. He carries with us our burdens, circumstances, temptations, and struggles with sin and old life patterns.

> Once you accept the Lord you are never going to be the same sinner again.

I am often asked: Why do we go back to our old ways at all? Even the Apostle Paul struggled with this in his own life. He confessed to us in Romans: "I know that nothing good lives in me, that is, in my sinful nature. For I have the desire to do what is good, but I cannot carry it out. For what I do is not the good I want to do; no, the evil I do not want to do—this I keep on doing. . . . What a wretched man I am! Who will rescue me from this body of death? Thanks be to God— through Jesus Christ our Lord!" (7:18–19, 24–25; paraphrased).

But why do we fail so often to put God first place in our lives? How can we stop? The advice Moses gave the Israelites in Deuteronomy 11 put very simply is: out with the old and in with the new. You have to *starve* the old you and *feed* the new you. You have to continually immerse yourself in the positive power of the Word of God. Moses tells them to *teach* the Word of God, *talk* the Word of

God, and *write* the Word of God. The Apostle Paul gave the same directive to the New Testament believers in Colossians.

Moses and Paul are telling us to fix the words of God onto our hearts and our minds. *Fix* means to embed, immerse, repair, and replace. It means get the Word of God, the Bible, so ingrained in your thinking that it dominates your thought processes. Having so immersed oneself in the Word of God, we are far more likely to keep Him foremost in our thoughts and in our actions. Unlike things of the world, God's Word is literally alive and fertile. If planted and cultivated, it can't help but bear fruit. Moses tells us how to do this.

Teach

Fix these words of mine in your hearts and minds; tie them as symbols on your hands and bind them on your foreheads.
Teach them to your children, talking about them when you sit at home and when you walk along the road, when you lie down and when you get up.

DEUTERONOMY 11:18–19

> Reading puts the Word into you. Teaching puts you personally into the Word.

It is said that teaching is the best education. Reading puts the Word into you. Teaching puts you personally into the Word. It is the beginning of doing the Word (James 1:22). You should be teaching God's words to your children for your sake and theirs. This, of course, will be hard to do if you never read them yourself and don't know them. We should all, therefore, have the habit of daily Bible study.

I have heard every excuse known to man for not reading the Bible. With all the excellent audio recordings available, even people who can't read are left with no excuse for not at least hearing the Word read and taught. I urge everyone to find a modern translation Bible and read it! I enjoy the New International Version arranged in chronological order and divided into 365 daily readings for my personal daily devotional. *The Message* Bible is also an easy-to-read and -understand modern translation.

There is nothing so life changing as preparing to teach the Word of God. You *will* be changed! You will see incredible things in the Word that you wouldn't discover any other way. Understanding and walking in God's Word is the source of flourishing in your life that arises from your new birth in Christ. The new birth is at the core of the command given in the above verse to fix God's Word in our hearts and minds. It changes us. And, as a testimony of this, the Israelites, and many Jews today, tied portions of scripture or *tefillin*, on their foreheads and weak arms as verse 18 prescribes.

The Apostle Paul said that he disciplined his body lest having preached the Word of God to others he himself might be found wanting in his personal habits (1 Corinthians 9:27). Some translations say Paul *beat* his body, meaning he sometimes had to be harsh with his natural will to keep it in submission. It is, of course, unlikely that Paul practiced self-flagellation and that the strong wording is meant to show how important Paul understood self-discipline to be. It is a sobering and life-changing experience to undertake the study of God's Word and to teach it to others.

If you were not taught the Word of God by your parents, how different might your life have been if they had? It is never too late to begin opening the Word to your children. Even if they are grown you can find appropriate occasions to share with them what you have learned. I urge you to find opportunities to absorb from others who regularly study the Word. Join a study group or an online study course. Studying and ministering the Word of God is the first and one of the best ways to put God first place in your life.

Talk

. . . admonish one another with all wisdom through psalms, hymns, and songs from the Spirit, singing to God with gratitude in your hearts.

COLOSSIANS 3:16

Talk about the Word of God at home and when you are on the road or everywhere you go. Interact with other believers about real-life applications of living by faith in God's promises. As you read and study the Word of God, begin to memorize scripture and incorporate Bible verses into your conversation. The wisdom of God's Word applies just as much today as it did when it was first inspired and written by the Holy Spirit.

I cannot count the many times I have drawn upon the Word in various business meetings. The Bible itself says, in Proverbs 25:11, a word aptly spoken is like apples of gold in settings of silver. Drawing on the Wisdom of the ages makes you look smarter too.

Even when you are alone, say positive Bible verses out loud to yourself. Learning science researchers have demonstrated that hearing your own voice speaking internalizes meaningful thoughts and information much more quickly than reading silently. How did you memorize that poem for high school English Lit class? You probably spoke it out loud over and over.

But something deeper happens when you hear God's Word. Paul taught in Romans: "Consequently, faith comes from hearing the message, and the message is heard through the word about Christ" (10:17). Somehow speaking the living Word of God opens a channel from your mind directly to your spirit where the power of faith resides. A miraculous transformation of your mind is deepened every time your mind hears you confessing the truth of God's Word. A number of years ago, I bought a radio alarm clock that also played cassettes. I taped myself reading positive scripture verses so the alarm I awoke to was my own voice reading God's Holy Word.

> A miraculous transformation of your mind is deepened every time your mind hears you confessing the truth of God's Word.

Develop a positive personal description of yourself, preferably incorporating a favorite scripture, so that you are ready any time you are asked: "How are you?". Instead of the usual fruitless, "Fine, thank you," you can respond with something like: "I am a blessed man of God!" or "The Lord is my Shepherd and I do not want for anything."

I sometimes embarrass my wife and others around me because I have not made a retail purchase in over twenty years without saying to the store clerk something like: "XX dollars? That is no problem because one thing I've got is money! My God blesses me abundantly above all I could ever hope or ask for." Or, I might say, "Yes, I am a lucky man! Why, my father owns all the cattle on a thousand hills." Or, "Yes, I give and it is given back to me pressed down and running over." Or, "The Lord God Almighty has made me the head and not the tail; I am above and not beneath the curse." You get the idea.

This practice isn't about showing off or ginning up faith *feelings*. Two very real things happen: First, I am speaking God's eternal truth into my life, affirming it's validity in my own experience so that, by faith, I know ever more deeply who I am in God's eyes. Second, responding to others in a faith-affirming way can open a door for further conversation and an opportunity to witness more deeply and personally. Talk to people. Don't preach, but talk from personal experience about God's love and trustworthiness. Whether you win them to Christ or not you are employing a powerful principle for yourself. Talking about God will deepen your faith and confidence in His Word. Daring to overcome the fear of talking about God in these ways is a bold act of putting Him first place in your life.

I can say with certainty the validity of God's Word has become my experience! The Bible plainly says that you will never the see the children of a righteous man begging bread. When I'm walking faithfully according to God's truth and principles I have never known want, even in the lean times. God has so wonderfully multiplied His blessing unto me. I have become rich in every way! I am not ashamed of it nor will I ever fail to thank Him for it. I firmly believe that applying the Promised Land principles in my life is a significant reason for it.

You never know what a timely word from you may do for someone. Some years ago, I had a downturn in my business (remember the Promised Land has both mountains and valleys.) One day, I was moping around my house feeling sorry for myself and one of my sons-in-law called to ask if he could borrow something—a lawn mower, I suppose. When he picked it up I asked him if he needed money for gas. "One thing I have is money!" was his reply. "What?" I was slightly taken aback. "Yeah," he said, "everyone at church is using your line now." I straightened my back, stuck out my chin, and said, "Bless God, nobody is going to steal my blessing!" I went straight into the house and went back to work.

Write

> *Write them on the door frames of your houses and on your gates, so that your days and the days of your children may be many . . .*

Deuteronomy 11:20–21

In Deuteronomy 11, God admonishes us to: "Fix these words of mine in your hearts and minds; tie them as symbols on your hands and bind them on your foreheads. . . Write them on the door frames of your houses and on your gates . . ." Spreading God's Truth around you in writing is a way of putting it in front of you at odd times when you are occupied with ordinary activities. It makes effortless the frequent memory of and grateful thoughts about God's love and the merciful gift of Jesus. I can walk down the hall of my home to fetch a hat from my closet and see a faith-affirming word that gives me a moment of grateful joy, and I breathe out, "Thank you, Jesus!" Let that happen here and there, fifty or a hundred times each day, and your spirit will become invincible to the darts and arrows of the enemy. I recommend you post favorite scriptures prominently in

> Get the Word of God visible to you to remind you continually about who you are.

your home and office. Buy artwork that incorporates inspiring Bible verses. Get the Word of God visible to you to remind you continually about who you are and what you believe.

Put scriptures inside your cabinets. Get a scripture a day calendar. I visited a home once where every room had its own dedication scripture framed and displayed prominently in the room. When the house was being built the owners wrote the same scriptures into the foundation before each room was built upon it.

Keep a journal. Write your thoughts in your Bible each day as you read it. Write out your prayers. Copy Bible passages of significance to you and carry them with you to read during ordinarily wasted times, like stop lights, doctor's waiting rooms, car pool lines, etc. I have used 3 x 5 index cards for this purpose and the practice has done as much to strengthen my faith outlook as any other spiritual discipline. I have seen studies that show we retain much more information we write down rather than merely read.

Not long after accepting the pastorate of RidgeLife Church, I delivered a sermon series entitled, "The Three Books You Should Bring to Church." They are: the Bible, of course, . . . your checkbook . . . and a journal to write in. I have kept notes on every sermon I have ever heard, most of them in specific journals for that purpose. Writing notes keeps the information fresh and it enables you to go back and study scripture references.

The Bottom Line

To obey principle number one: "Love the LORD your God with all your heart and all your soul and all your strength," very likely you are going to have to *do* something to make that happen. You are going to have to *change* and stay changed. The Bible says of itself that *it*, the *Word*, is sharper than any two-edged sword. It is how God reveals Himself to us. We cannot love God as He deserves if we do not know Him. How then can we know Him if we do not know His Word that He gave to reveal Himself?

I know well from experience in these matters because I was really messed up as a new believer. I had to employ all these measures because I didn't want to stay messed up. It also took me a long time to overcome the desire of my flesh to live out my old ways. But I can report that you can succeed. Praise God, you put Him first and He will preserve you, and you will get to a place of peace and rest.

May I respectfully add that you don't get to make the rules. You may say you love God but then say you are just not a reader and thus never read His Word. This, of course, puts you in a horrible position to defend your faith when called upon to do so, much less lead someone to Christ. As a consequence, you do not teach or even speak of His Word. No, you must put God first above yourself and grow up to do that which He commands. Commitment, even out of love, usually involves discipline. But growing up means commitment to God no longer feels like discipline. It becomes a daily celebration of the true glory of life. In putting God first and loving Him above all else, you will learn what it means to be truly free.

Principle #2
Idolatry Forbidden

You Can't Love Your Dog More Than Your Neighbor.

---

*You saw no form of any kind the day the LORD spoke to you at
Horeb out of the fire. Therefore watch yourselves very carefully, so
that you do not become corrupt and make for yourselves an idol,
an image of any shape, whether formed like a man or a woman, or
like any animal on earth or any bird that flies in the air, or like any
creature that moves along the ground or any fish in the waters below.
And when you look up to the sky and see the sun, the moon and the
stars—all the heavenly array—do not be enticed into bowing down to
them and worshipping things the LORD your God has apportioned to
all the nations under heaven.*

Deuteronomy 4:15–19

*Although they claimed to be wise, they became fools and exchanged
the glory of the immortal God for images made to look like a mortal*

human being and birds and animals and reptiles. Therefore God gave
them over in the sinful desires of their hearts to sexual impurity for the
degrading of their bodies with one another. They exchanged the truth
about God for a lie, and worshipped and served created things rather
than the Creator—who is forever praised. Amen.

ROMANS 1:22–25

In the beginning God created the heavens and the earth.

GENESIS 1:1

In the opening pages of the Bible a war is underway—a war of words; a war of religions. Many biblical scholars believe that when Moses related the creation story in Genesis he was putting forth more than an account of how God created the heavens and the earth. Genesis chapter 1 is also a *polemic*, which is a passionate and strongly worded argument against someone or something. In this case, it was a declaration that God created the heavens and the earth separate from Himself, and an argument against the pagan cultures of Moses' day.

Idolatry is worshipping something other than the One True God who made all things, or putting something above your obedience and devotion to God. The word *idolatry* conjures an image of pagan religions worshipping statues of stone animals and the like. While worshipping graven images may be a medium through which we see this perversion practiced, one does not have to worship a graven image to live in idolatry.

In the very first sentence of the Bible Moses was saying to the world: "Egyptians, the sun may be what you believe is god but it is God who made the sun who should be worshipped." "Babylonians, you may worship the moon but it is God who made the moon." The Egyptians worshipped the sun, Pharaoh (a man), various animals, the cobra, and even the Nile River. The Phoenicians lived by the sea and their god was represented by a fish. The Babylonians worshipped the moon and the stars. The Canaanites worshipped Moloch, represented by the form of a man with a bull's head. To earn the blessing of Moloch, the Canaanites burned alive one or more of their small children in a public sacrificial fire.

All these nations and religions incorporated an inappropriate veneration of the earth, its natural cycles, animals, or astrological observations. Astrology (predicting future events through astronomical observations) was wide spread. Polytheism (worshipping multiple deities) was common. Ancestor worship is widespread in the history of tribes and civilizations around the globe. All of these practices are an unholy perversion of faith, which denies the truth that God created all things in the universe but is *not part* of His creation.

Moses, writing with direct revelation of God, said *NO!* God, the One True God, is without form. God created the universe and all that is within it. The Sun, the moon, the stars, and the animals . . . all things were created by Him. The earth's cycles, everything in nature—He created it all. Mankind is to worship Him alone. There is obvious evidence of God's existence and power in creation but none of his essence. This is what Paul condemned in Romans chapter 1 about worshipping the creature rather than the Creator (v. 25).

So what has this got to do with me and getting more promise out of the Promised Land? And, how is this different from Principle #1 Love the Lord your God? In Genesis, Moses tells us we must worship the truth and not a lie. GOD CREATED THE UNIVERSE. You are not a cosmic accident! Faith believes this down to the core. God alone is worthy of worship as God. Worship of anything in God's creation is idolatry and God hates it. This includes anything in creation, but especially mankind or anything men create. The most common idolatry of all is worship of self. The man who holds back a tithe to finance a personal want is worshipping himself above his acknowledgement that God is the source of his increase. The woman who dresses in revealing clothes and excessive makeup to display her sexual attractiveness is worshipping herself instead of the God who would have her consider how her appearance can harm or bless others.

> The most common idolatry of all is worship of self.

NOTHING and NO ONE BUT GOD is worthy of worship. This is a vitally important principle for successful living in the Promised Land. You must, above all things, know that you are created by God for the high purpose of having fellowship with Him. Anything that dilutes or perverts your understanding and practice of this principle will dilute or pervert your potential in the Promised Land. God makes this clear again and again throughout His dealings with Israel and in His Word through the New Testament writers. It is God's last word about you. You were made for Him.

Don't Mix, Don't Mingle

As we read Old Testament history, some of it sounds harsh to our modern ears. God's instructions to the Israelites to go into the Promised Land and utterly destroy its inhabitants seems so very . . . un-Godlike. We don't instinctively know how to apply these stories today.

There is a very simple way, however, to interpret these scriptures for us: God is telling you and me, just as He told the Israelites, to not make treaties with idolatrous people; don't mix with them, don't marry them, in fact, have nothing at all to do with them. They are far more likely to dilute or pervert your faith than you are to change them.

"I don't know any idolatrous people," you might say. Oh, yes you do! Anyone who denies the truth of God is engaged in a form of idolatry because, by definition, they are putting their daily trust in something other than God. This clarity must be in the front of your mind when you interact with non-believers at work, at school, in your family, and elsewhere. Does that mean we cannot evangelize the world? Of course not! As you are resolute in your faith, grounded in prayer, and directed by the Holy Spirit, share your faith aggressively. Aren't we supposed to be a light on a candlestick? Absolutely!!! Keep it that way.

> Idolatry is putting your daily trust in something other than God.

But even some Christians mistakenly think they can innocently toy with blatantly idolatrous things and not be affected by them.

"Have nothing to do with idolaters" doesn't mean you don't minister to them or love them. It means don't even be a bystander when they dabble in astrology, spiritualism, Wicca, New-Age philosophy, etc. Don't play games with such things that lure others with hints of truth. They are false religions and lies and are an offense to your God.

Have you ever engaged in Astrology by reading your horoscope in the paper? Have you ever engaged in fortune telling by getting your palm read? Have you ever engaged in spiritualism by taking part in a séance? They may seem like innocent things at the time, but they are lures fishing for men's hearts. I repeat: Don't play games with this stuff. Your God is a jealous god and, for your sakes, He will not be gentle with your adulterous affairs with other gods.

Secular Humanism Is Idolatry

We have in our midst perhaps one of the most pervasive and insidious forms of idolatry in the history of mankind. Secular Humanism denies or ignores a Creator and thus anything in creation as *intentionally* created. It specifically rejects religious dogma and supposes that humans are inherently or innately good and moral beings without the need for such a code from a supreme being; which begs the question: Parents, do you have to teach your children to be good? The answer is: Of course!

Secular Humanism is subtly taught to every student in public education from pre-K all the way through college. As the ideological basis of our government education system, it is fast *becoming* our basis for governance as well. The guardians of political correctness will not allow a Christian worldview to be discussed alongside secular humanism. Unlike earlier times in America, it is now improper and even impolite outside of a church venue, to propose policies, viewpoints, or judgments; teach history, ethics, economics, humanities, etc.; or even run for office under the banner of biblical faith.

In the worldview of secular humanism, there is no God and thus no Creation. There are only accidental collisions of atoms that exist because of processes not *yet* fully understood by science. God and the Bible hold no ultimate truth. Science (an otherwise beneficial discipline of man) becomes, in the religion of secular humanism, the only source of ultimate truth. It is, again, the works of man that are worshipped. The ethics of man become relative to time, place, person, and/or situation. There are no universal absolute rights and wrongs and all living things have equal value. Despite exalting Man and our ability to reason, we are considered mere accidents of nature with no greater value than animals with whom we are allegedly equal.

This thinking spawns a wide variety of modern social phenomena, which, in my mind, are forms of idolatry. Since secular humanism denies both a Creator and a Creation, the only other explanation for life available is random, purposeless evolution. We are merely animal descendants of simpler animal forms. Because we humans depend on the health of the environment and not the other way around, the environment is elevated to almost godlike status and thus more important than the people who occupy it. Earth worship is very popular and chic among opinion makers and Hollywood types.

I remember an old Imperials song, which had a line: "the latest rage is to reason things out . . ." Secular humanism denies the veracity

> Secular humanism is a tool of the devil designed for one purpose: to get your eyes off God and onto yourselves.

of scripture in favor of human reason. Our moral code, sense of justice, and our ethical values are not based upon the ethics of Jesus Christ and His Holy Word. Society at large is in the process of exchanging the Truth of God for a lie from the pit of hell.

I do not look for demons around every corner, nor do I assign a demon to every bad habit. But secular humanism is a tool of the devil designed for one purpose: to get your eyes off God and onto yourselves. It is there to sow seeds of doubt and unbelief—that there is no heaven and no hell. There is no God and certainly no need for a savior. The impact of this worldview has been devastating to Western civilization. We will now look at a couple of its most prominent and damaging expressions in our culture.

The Sacrificial Alter of Choice

How great is the stain from the blood of our unborn babies sacrificed upon the altar of convenience? Have we not made ourselves gods when we say that we have the right to determine who lives and who dies on the basis of "a woman's right to choose?" What arrogance we display to presume we have such a choice to make!

Actually, the only way one can make such an argument is to deny the truth of each and every human being's potential to relate to their Heavenly Father. No matter the cost, no matter the inconvenience, no matter the hardship, every human being is a created being. Every human being has a soul and a spirit. We are NOT animals. We are NOT gods.

Do not be deluded in your thinking. The Canaanites were expelled from the Promised Land because of their idolatrous practices. Most horrible among those abominations, as I explained above, were the sacrifices of their children to the god Moloch. Are we not engaged in the same practices? The Canaanites sacrificed their children in order to preserve their prosperity, presumably by honoring Moloch above even a treasured child. Abortions are usually performed because a pregnancy is inconvenient and an economic or lifestyle threat. In other words, abortion is the sacrifice of a child's life to preserve one's prosperity, presumably by honoring oneself above the child. Read to the words of Ezekiel:

Therefore, you prostitute, hear the word of the LORD! This is what the Sovereign LORD says: Because you poured out your lust and exposed your naked body in your promiscuity with your lovers, and because of all your detestable idols, and because you gave them your children's blood, therefore I am going to gather all your lovers, with whom you found pleasure, those you loved as well as those you hated. I will gather them against you from all around and will strip you in front of them, and they will see you stark naked. I will sentence you to the punishment of women who commit adultery and who shed blood; I will bring on you the blood vengeance of my wrath and jealous anger.

EZEKIEL 16:35–38; EMPHASIS ADDED

God cannot and will not condone the practice of abortion. We as a society have blood on our hands if we do not oppose the practice. Killing a viable human fetus is killing a viable human being. You cannot argue the truth of that statement away.

That is not to say He will not forgive those who repent of it. This like any other sin can be forgiven. If you or anyone you know has fallen to that temptation confess it and seek the forgiveness of our Lord and Savior. God wants to restore you and fellowship with you. I personally believe you will meet that child in heaven if you do.

Radical Environmentalism and Radical Animal Rights Activism

The most radical environmental activists believe you are no better than a rat or, alternatively, a rat is just as important as you. They care more about the survivability of obscure insects than of fellow humans who are in need. We allow hundreds of thousands of people to die from malaria every year rather than risk endangering the ecosystem with a proven mosquito control agent. We applaud when no animals were used in the testing of products that could protect our health or even save lives.

Animal rights activists engage in idolatry when they deny God and equate humans with animals. Extremist environmentalism sometimes seek to put humans and animals on the same moral and social footing. These individuals would seek to end all use of animals by humans for any purpose and to equate any such use as exploitation. The Bible clearly teaches, however, that humans were created separately and distinctly from animals. Yet radical animal rights activists often trade the truth of God's word for a lie:

I'm not only uninterested in having children. I am opposed to having children. Having a purebred human baby is like having a purebred dog; it is nothing but vanity, human vanity. (Ingrid Newkirk, PETA's founder and president)[2]

Surely there will be some nonhuman animals whose lives, by any standards, are more valuable than the lives of some humans. (Peter Singer, Animal Liberation)[3]

There are even a few among the most radical animal rights activists (such as Gary Yourofsky, founder of Animals Deserve Absolute Protection Today and Tomorrow), who express a strong desire to see *extreme* physical harm come to hunters, fur consumers, and others they consider to be uncaring of animal suffering.[4]

The majority of animal rights advocates, though just as emotionally committed to their cause, wouldn't advocate Yourofsky's extreme views of violence against humans.

But without a biblical context for creation, the values shared almost universally by animal rights advocates result in a form of idolatry that dethrones God's rulership of creation and elevates human perspectives as a final word—perhaps I should say *certain* human perspectives. Ironically, the "superior human perspective" of animal rights activists isn't as much an elevation of *value* for *animals* as a *diminishment* of *human* value.

How God's heart must be broken when he hears his children speak so poorly of His most beloved creation: themselves. The

> How God's heart must be broken when he hears his children speak so poorly of His most beloved creation: themselves.

great sin here is to deny God, His Word, and our ability to live in fellowship with Him. No one in their right mind can abide cruelty to animals but most animal rights activists assign more rights to animals than to humans in general and none to unborn human babies!

Radical environmentalism is described thusly by Wikipedia: "The radical environmental movement aspires to what scholar Christopher Manes calls 'a new kind of environmental activism: iconoclastic, uncompromising, discontented with traditional conservation policy, at time illegal . . .'" "Radical environmentalism presupposes a need to reconsider Western ideas of religion and philosophy (including capitalism, patriarchy and globalization) sometimes through 'resacralising' and reconnecting with nature."[5]

"Resacralising" means to make the Earth sacred and is the oldest form of idolatry known to human kind. So called "New Age" devotion to Earth worship would be better referred to as Old Age religion. Virtually all early pagan cultures incorporated some form of Earth worship that persists to this day in the form of our modern notions of Mother Earth. Inappropriate veneration of our planet is, however, . . . inappropriate! God has clearly communicated to us his displeasure in this regard.

The plain fact is that one does not have to omit God the Creator of the Earth in order to appreciate His creation and desire to protect it. The simple fact that He did create it ought to foster an appropriate sense of stewardship in each of us. Our first job on planet Earth was to tend the garden. We, however, must keep our priorities crystal clear: God is God and Earth is not.

God help us, for our idolatry and unbelief!

Lest We Point Fingers

I admit I am no longer a pet person, which, for some, disqualifies me from talking about how people live with their pets. But I do think the attention and place given to some pets seem out of proportion with biblical values and sometimes perhaps even crosses the line into idolatry. And this is one place where we Christians can get a little humanistically fuzzy in our thinking. We tend, for example, to attribute human qualities to our pets. We tend to believe our pets have the capacity to love us as we love them. We really can sometimes love our dogs and cats more than our neighbors. Most pets in the United States live better than many people in the world, and that's no exaggeration. We have huge pet stores, pet spas, gourmet pet food, and designer pet clothes and bedding. As Christians, we should be disturbed that our dog lives better than our neighbors, but often we see no disproportion in this.

Then there is the question that is so often posed to me: Will my dog go to heaven? I ask back (if the asker is an adult), "Excellent question!! Do wolves? How about vultures? Maybe grizzly bears? Why not? They are all carrion eaters just like dogs. If your dog has an eternal soul then it stands to reason that all animals do, doesn't it?" We are not superior, then, to even a garden slug if you are going to pursue that line of logic. In stark contrast, however, Revelations 22:15 says "Outside [of heaven] are the dogs, those who practice magic arts, the sexually immoral, the murderers, the idolaters and everyone who loves and practices falsehood." The direct meaning is that no unclean thing will be in heaven and dogs are very much considered unclean in Middle Eastern cultures.

In fairness, only God is the arbitrator of who or what goes to heaven. In fact, as a horse lover, I am encouraged that the Bible mentions horses in heaven (2 Kings 2:11–12). I suppose if your pet gives you great peace, for all I know, God may allow you its company in heaven. The point, however, is that God's Word is only clear about humans having an eternal soul. You were created,

> You were created for God, your dog was created for you.

according to the Bible, above the animals and just a little below the angels. You, not your dog, were created for the expressed purpose of having fellowship with God. Your dog was created to have fellowship with you.

So why even ask if animals have eternal souls? What difference would it make to know for sure if they do or don't? Would the answer affect how we understand God's work in our lives and in history? If so, can you see that such concern would be idolatrous or very close to it? Many unnecessary, distracting questions and concerns like this have crept into our thinking and affected how we look at the world. With all the otherwise wonderful comforts and convenience Western materialism has brought, we have allowed them to reshape our values and dilute our understanding and appreciation of who we are in Christ

No, we must take a stand here. I am a child of my Father, the most high God. Jesus died for me! My sins are forgiven! I was uniquely created to enjoy the fruits of a unique relationship with the Creator of the Universe. My Father is the Great I Am, and I will not suffer fools who try to tell me I'm just an animal or an animal is just like me.

Naturally, I don't condone abuse of animals any more than I condone pollution and poor stewardship of the environment. We are to protect and nurture the earth and all life upon it as gifts from God. But the earth is not our mother. It is our servant created to equip our service to God. If it will find a cure for cancer, I say any amount of animal testing to save one human life is reasonable.

> The earth is not our mother. It is our servant created to equip our service to God.

Another form of benign fuzzy thinking we can encounter is "Positive Thinking." You may have heard it said, however, "If it is to be . . . it is up to me," or "I am the master of my fate and the captain of my soul." These kinds of catchy phrases are often heard as song lyrics or movie dialog and are a constant influence to our thinking. They are idolatrous to the degree that they promote self worship and independence from God. This kind of thinking, too, is widespread and weakens the firm foundations of God's truth our culture once stood upon.

I'm not saying we should not have a healthy self-esteem; we are, after all, children of the Most High God. We need to know explicitly who we are in Christ Jesus, which can and should be more liberating and empowering than self-reliance. In fact, the greatest barrier most of us have to overcome is self-degradation. So often we have such a hard time appreciating who we are. We have royal blood in our veins. We are sons and daughters of the King.

Bottom Line

We must get it straight in our thinking and be resolute to reject idolatry in our midst and in our hearts. We are not mere animal products of the earth. We are men and women created in God's image. As a man or woman in Christ, you are a child of the Most High God. You can trust Him to lead you. He has great and wonderful blessings in store for you. And if you are diligent in your calling and faithful to all God's principles there is nothing to prevent your success in this world. But you must keep straight Who God is, who you are, and what everything else in creation is if you want more promise out of the Promised Land.

CHAPTER SIX

PRINCIPLE #3 THE TEN COMMANDMENTS

Get Back to Basics of Life

Then the LORD spoke to you out of the fire. You heard the sound of words but saw no form; there was only a voice. He declared to you his covenant, the Ten Commandments, which he commanded you to follow and then wrote them on two stone tablets. And the LORD directed me at that time to teach you the decrees and laws you are to follow in the land that you are crossing the Jordan to possess.

DEUTERONOMY 4:12–14

So be careful to do what the LORD your God has commanded you; do not turn aside to the right or to the left. Walk in obedience to all that the LORD your God has commanded you, so that you may live and prosper and prolong your days in the land that you will possess.

DEUTERONOMY 5:32–33

God encourages Israel's obedience numerous times in the Old Testament, as in Deuteronomy chapter 5. But thankfully, rather than commanding blind obedience God provides wonderful promises, such as the very sweeping, grand promises in Deuteronomy chapter 28 for those who will live in His Promised Land according to His commands. God promises they will be blessed, their children will be blessed, their work will be blessed, their land and storehouses will be blessed, and He will grant abundant prosperity, and even that their enemies will be defeated (vs. 3–12; paraphrased). God then finishes this litany with a remarkable statement in verse 13: "The Lord will make you the head, not the tail. If you pay attention to the commands of the LORD your God that I give you this day and carefully follow them, you will always be at the top, never at the bottom." Then God again commands obedience to His Law as being linked to these blessings (v. 14–15).

The Ten Commandments are a beautiful and profound gift from God. Thomas Cahill said it best in the subtitle of his wonderful book, *The Gifts of the Jews*. The Ten Commandments ". . . changed the way everyone thinks and feels."[6] The Ten Commandments serve as the foundation of our Judeo-Christian heritage, which, in turn, is the foundation of not just the United States, but all of Western civilization.

> Make no mistake about it. Ours is a Judeo/Christian nation.

Make no mistake about it. Ours is a Judeo/Christian nation. I know it has become fashionable to debate and, for the most part, deny this fundamental truth; but the Ten Commandments are so ingrained in our thinking and moral life and are so great an influence on every aspect of our society that even the most ardent atheists can't escape living by the social ethics framed by them. They have to explain the persistence of these ethics and their own adherence to them in sociological and evolutionary terms, but the point is made every time they obey them. Our society is built upon biblical foundations and biblical law.

The world into which God gave His commandments was strange and hostile beyond our understanding. One day, as I was working on this project I became aware of a song playing on the radio. It was *The Circle of Life* by Elton John from the Disney movie *The Lion King*. It's a beautiful song that, nevertheless, could describe the bizarre world before the very revolutionary gift of The Ten Commandments.

The *circle of life* is a foundational worldview through which most of the world's ancient pagan societies understood nature and spirituality. It says that nothing changes; everything is bound up into the cycles of nature. Nature and the cosmos are themselves god or, most commonly, creation is ordered by numerous gods, usually impersonal, that are associated with one part or attribute of nature. But in contrast to the biblical worldview in which God created all things separate from Himself, in all pagan societies spirit and matter are inseparable. The concept of future typically went no further than the completed seasons of the year. Humans had very little individual worth, if any. This world view had enormous impact on the ethics and morality of its adherents. In some parts of the world today it still does.

Under pagan cycles of existence, people did not possess individual human rights. The worth of a person wasn't in who he was as an individual but in what family or tribe he was a part of, or whom he belonged to. A majority of the world's population was enslaved to a minority. And this never changed because change was not seen as natural. Everything and all circumstances recurred over and over and were written in nature.

The moon and Earth and their cycles were often venerated through bizarre sexual orgies intended to glorify the cycles of birth and death. Sometimes it culminated in the death of the "worshipper" through sacrifice by the priests or priestesses with whom they had "worshipped." Human sacrifice was a relatively common aspect of paganism since the material plane was seen as inferior to the spiritual. Refusing to sacrifice, or be one, was seen as regarding oneself or material life as higher than the gods. As is common with worldly systems though, the powerful were seldom pressed to prove their devotion unless they fell into a ruler's disfavor.

But the ordinary human was born to follow in his father's footsteps. No different future for him was imaginable than that his father lived. There was no such thing as opportunity for a mere commoner to rise above his station in life.

It simply was not a function of the circle of life. To even have such an idea one must believe things can change—that history can open new paths that lead to the unknown and things never before experienced was a foreign concept. If the world had always been covered with nothing but ocean and we had been created by God to dwell in floating vessels built from floating debris, would any person ever conceive of the existence of dry ground? Suggesting the idea would be like trying to explain colors to a person totally blind from birth. It's the same for peoples who were and are stuck in cycle-of-life paganism.

Unfortunately, we can't understand paganism as something that happened only in ancient times. Perhaps half the world still lives under original pagan systems although many of them such as some varieties in India are now experiencing conflict with their ideals due to the growing influence of western pragmatism and democracy. We should be very careful not to be smug about the many ways our civilization has been blessed by our foundation upon the Ten Commandments. But there is a reason that today there are skyscrapers in New York and suicide bombers in the Middle East. There is a reason why infanticide of baby girls is common in Asian countries where girls are less desired than boys. It is because many Asian and Middle Eastern societies lack the nobility that arises out of the Ten Commandments for all who embrace them. In our society, however, there are finishing schools where girls are taught to believe in themselves and women, in general, have increasingly gained equality because of the moral influence of the Ten Commandments.

Radical Islam and other Eastern religions discount the value of the individual in favor of the community or family. It is much easier to recruit persons to commit suicide who see no real future for themselves on earth. They are so convinced about the glory awaiting them in heaven for their sacrifice versus their life's potential here on earth, that they fearlessly heed the call of self-destruction by a "holy man." Honor killings are permissible if one's child dishonors the family by straying from orthodox doctrine. The individual has no worth, a limited future, and is unable to break out of the caste of one's birth. There is no future different from the present. All of this is so foreign to our Western Judeo-Christian mindset that we have difficulty imagining it.

What do you think would happen if Billy Graham announced a holy *jihad*? Or the U.S. Army had a training camp for suicide bombers? We are culturally incapable of comprehending such thoughts, much less act on them. And yet, if atheists are right then ultimately all things are permissible if they're profitable to our interests. But atheists and self-proclaimed pagans in America don't live that way, do they? All of us in what was once called Christendom still possess an inner core of restraint born of our biblically-based instincts. Criminals who violate those moral restraints may have no remorse but they know why their actions are wrong.

> Our civilization was born that night Abraham heard the voice of the One True God.

Because of the Ten Commandments, because of the Jew, we can aspire to change our circumstances and ourselves. The way we think, the way we feel, our senses of justice, of creativity, of connectivity, and communication with our Creator were all born the evening Abraham looked up into the heavens and, instead of seeing the moon as god, heard the voice of the One True God. When Moses ascended the mountain of God and received the Ten Commandments written out by the hand of God, Western civilization was codified.

There is no document, in all the literatures of the world, like the Ten Commandments. These are direct, simple, elevating, and equalizing principles by which to live. Ancient societies did develop ethical guidelines or sets of laws but they tended to be pragmatic or proverbial in nature (if you want to lead a happy life you should do such-and-such or avoid this-or-that).

On Mount Horeb, for the first time since the Garden of Eden, human beings are given a verbal code of law directly from the Creator without justification or qualification. It is simply: Thus says the Lord our God. It is a thunderous and yet uncomplicated law; THOU SHALL or SHALL NOT. They are not suggestions or challenges. As Thomas Cahill concludes, the Ten Commandments ". . . require no justification nor can they be argued away."[7] I would add: Nor can they be ignored without consequence. They were written by the hand of God from within the fire and smoke of Mount Sinai and have been received as reasonable, necessary, and unalterable by billions since that day.

One might think to add or subtract from the Ten Commandments, but they are complete and unalterable. They are so complete that what sanctions they do not emphasize explicitly can, with wisdom, be deduced from those that are. They are elegantly simple. These commandments are easy to repeat and easy to learn. And though we as a human race have never kept them perfectly, we can envision a far better world were we to do so.

The era into which these commands were given by God were barbarous beyond our comprehension. The Jews were a very short time from having escaped the brutality of slavery. These words were not spoken to a king in his palace, but to a shepherd and his people while encamped in the desert at the base of a barren mountain. These commandments steeled these people with unassailable Truth and equipped them to change history itself.

Lastly, another of the profound and revolutionary aspects of the Ten Commandments is that they made all men everywhere equals because they are ubiquitous. All men answer to this law equally and through them all men have equal access before their Creator. The law gives all people the same rights and protections for the first time since Eden. It is always wrong to steal, no matter who you are or from whom you are stealing.

> The Ten Commandments give every individual worth, value, equality, and a future.

The Ten Commandments give every individual worth, value, equality, and a future. They leveled the playing field for all who came under them and called for strict change in the fundamental worldview and social ethic of society. That means any change became possible, and with it any future with only God's power to bless as a limit. Though it took generations for these concepts to soak into our DNA and make us who we are today, the concepts of self-determination and self-actualization were born that night in the desert so long ago and so far away.

Our Lord Jesus Christ would say, even 2000 years later, His words recorded in Matthew's Gospel:

Think not that I am come to destroy the law, or the prophets:
I am not come to destroy, but to fulfil. For verily I say unto you,
Till heaven and earth pass, one jot or one tittle shall in no wise
pass from the law, till all be fulfilled. Whosoever therefore shall break
one of these least commandments, and shall teach men so, he shall be
called the least in the kingdom of heaven: but whosoever shall do and
teach them, the same shall be called great in the kingdom of heaven.

MATTHEW 5:17–19; KJV

Approximately 1,700 years after our Lord affirmed The Ten Commandments, their principles were embodied in the founding documents of this great nation of ours.

We hold these truths to be self-evident, that all men are created equal,
that they are endowed by their Creator with certain unalienable
rights, that among these are Life, Liberty, and the Pursuit of
Happiness.

CONSTITUTION OF THE UNITED STATES, ARTICLE 1

There are those who will dispute me in this, but as for me and my house it is forever settled. Not just the United States of America but the entirety of Western civilization rest upon the Judeo-Christian principles embodied in the Ten Commandments and God's Holy Word.

Several thousand years after being given the Ten Commandments, it is hard for us in our modern times to view them as radical and transforming. For many they are a dusty set of do's and don'ts from a kill-joy God on a puffy cloud; but they radically altered the course of human history. The Ten Commandments:

1. opened to all people everywhere for all time the opportunity to relate to the One True and Living God
2. made all men equal for the first time because they apply to all men equally
3. granted basic human rights for the first time
4. established and codified private property rights

Imagine, if you can, an entire people so long enslaved and then miraculously freed and gloriously given and embracing a code that is destined to set all men free? The Ten Commandments can be grouped in a variety of ways and some scholarly debate exists about the exact number of groups. But for our purposes we can view them as two groups of five. They are enumerated in Deuteronomy 5:6–21.

Vertical Law

The first five Commandments govern our vertical relationships— that is our relationships with God and our parents:

1) "You shall have no other gods before me . . ." v. 7

This Command is preceded by "I am the Lord your God who brought you out of the Land of Egypt, from the house of slavery . . ." and for the Jews the goal of this redemption was for them to be His people and to hold complete belief in Him. This command is directed, however, not just to the Jew but to all men to believe in the existence of God and His influence on events in the world. Further, it prohibits belief in or worship of any additional deities. It is from this commandment that our First Principle arises: Thou shalt love the Lord thy God with all thy heart and all thy might.

2) "You shall not make for yourself an [idol] . . ." v. 8
This command specifically enumerates not making *graven images* (or models of gods) that one might worship. But it goes further to prohibit the worship of the products of Creation. We have already discussed these first two commandments in great detail in the previous chapters.

3) "You shall not misuse the name of the LORD your God . . ." v. 11
This command is to never take the name of the Lord in vain. Most commonly we hear this in the context of "do not swear or cuss using the Lord's name." As if it is "OK" to utter profanities otherwise. It is amazing to me the many ways that both God's and Jesus' names have been conjoined with swear words in modern colloquial English. Even relatively *safe* expressions such as "golly" or "gosh darn" are sanitized versions of their unspeakable counterparts. Undoubtedly, it is always wrong to use God's name in any form of a curse word, but I hear people often say "God!!" or "Jesus!!" as to express disdain or anger so as to render these words curses. This is specifically forbidden, as well it should be, and completely unbecoming toward our Creator and Savior.

We also understand this commandment to not blaspheme the name of God. To blaspheme is to slander the character of God or to speak impiously or irreverently of God. It is to profane His name through irreverence or contempt. Blaspheme can also take the form of ascribing to God unbiblical attributes, emotions, or predilections such as saying, "God hates sinners!"

But in biblical terms, this commandment means that we ought not abuse the name of God. Often that is described as swearing falsely or using His name in pointless or insincere oaths. There are, however, numerous examples in the Old Testament and a few in the New Testament where God's name is called upon in oaths to tell the truth or to support the truth of the statement being sworn to. The books of Daniel and Revelation include instances where an angel sent by God invokes the name of God to support the truth of apocalyptic revelations. God himself is presented as swearing by His own name ("As surely as I live . . .") to guarantee the certainty of various events foretold through the prophets. Witnesses in a trial affirm their veracity by placing their hand on a Bible and swearing truthfulness with, "So help me God."

The Hebrew word translated as "in vain" also means "emptiness, vanity; emptiness of speech, lying." The Hebrew word translated "take" means "to lift, carry, bear, take, take away." The expression "to take in vain" is also translated less literally as "to misuse in any way." Some have interpreted the commandment to be against perjury, since invoking God's name in an oath was considered a guarantee of the truth of a statement or promise. Other scholars believe the original intent was to prohibit using God's name in magic spells, incantations, or other pagan rituals.

To avoid being guilty of accidently blaspheming the name of God, Jewish scholars will not utter or write the formal name of God. I have a Messianic Rabbi friend who will write "God" as "G-D" and will refer to Him most times in prayer as "Abba." Other names such as "Adonai," which is translated "Lord" in English, will be also used instead.

For us today, this command-ment means to always be reverent and respectful in all our references to Him and all we do in His name. He is, after all, God, the Creator of the Universe. I think a little respect is due Him to whom we owe our existence.

> Be reverent and respectful in all our references to God and all we do in His name.

4) "Observe the Sabbath day by keeping it holy . . ." v. 12

In Hebrew, Deuteronomy uses the term *shamor*, which means "to guard." The word "Sabbath" refers to rest. The term "Sabbath" derives from the Hebrew *Shabbat*, "to cease," which was first used in the biblical account of the seventh day of Creation (Genesis 2:2–3). To "sabbath" is the act of resting because God rested on the seventh day after creating the Universe and everything in it during the pre-vious six days. Physical resting refers most often to a rest day, but can refer to sabbathing or resting for other periods of time such as a Sabbath year when the soil rested.

The seventh day of the week, therefore, is holy and its holiness was to be guarded. Just as God ceased from the work of Creation, so, too, is man to cease from his labors. The Jews viewed this com-mand as to completely abstain from productive activity or work on the Sabbath Day and to use the day to worship their Creator. Here again was one of the great equalizing Commandments; all were to rest, even the beasts of burden.

Heretofore, there was no such thing. It was completely unimaginable to not work every day. With this command God invented the weekend!—In the process, recreation or re-creation. Man could now rest, study, enjoy a day of contemplation, recharge, pray, think, create, prepare on a deeper heart level, and, most of all, acknowledge with our obedient rest that all our days are given by God. The quantum effect was to advance civilization as never before. Now, there was a day to go to church . . . and play golf afterwards! First and foremost, however, it is a day to dedicate oneself to godly pursuits and, above all else, attend church!

For the Jew, the Sabbath remains a critically important weekly holy day. While on a trip to Jerusalem recently, I was amazed to see many Jewish families have a very formal and dressy dinner on Friday night. Then, starting that evening, the hotel set most of the elevators to open on every floor so that observant Jews need not punch the button as that electrical transmission would constitute "making fire." Saturday was very uneventful as most shops and restaurants were closed. But Saturday night was a party with people out in the streets celebrating life all over again.

Most Christians look upon the Sabbath more "in spirit" than through the application of complete rest from all physical activity. And we, for the most part, observe the first day of the week (Sunday) as our Sabbath rather than the seventh day. Our response to the Sabbath ought to be sincere: Go to church and worship God there first and foremost. Give God the glory He is due and rest in His peace and provision for our lives.

5) "Honor your father and your mother . . ." v. 16

This command is the first command with a direct promise . . ." So that you may live long and prosper." Also, keeping this law was associated with the ability of the nation of Israel to remain in the land to which God was leading them. The Jews felt that the obligation to honor one's parents is an obligation that one owes to God. You fulfill this obligation to God through your actions toward your parents. Dishonoring parents by striking or cursing them was punishable by death. According to the prophet Malachi, God makes the analogy himself: "A son honors his father, and a slave his master. If I am a father, where is the honor due me? (Malachi 1:6).

There is a presumption within this commandment that parents will lead the next generation and set appropriate examples for them; that they will conduct themselves lawfully and scripturally. It is upon this basis that Jesus and the apostles affirmed this commandment in their teachings. As related in Matthew 19:17–19 and Mark 10:17–19, Jesus noted the Fifth Commandment when reciting general lists of the qualities of righteous living to the rich young ruler. Paul quotes this commandment to the church in Ephesus in his letter to them in chapter 6.

Furthermore, there is evidence that adult children were expected to provide material support to elderly parents. Jesus, while on the Cross, asked the Apostle John to care for His mother, a responsibility which he accepted. Paul advised Timothy: "But if a widow has children or grandchildren, these should learn first of all to put their religion into practice by caring for their own family and so repaying their parents and grandparents, for this is pleasing to God" 1 Timothy 5:4.

However, there is no requirement that children exalt their parents over God, meaning the primacy of the First Commandment would rule if in conflict. Children were not required to follow their parents into sin. In fact, quite the opposite; Jesus challenged His followers to leave mother and father, house and home if need be, to follow Him. "He who loves father or mother more than Me is not worthy of Me. And he who loves son or daughter more than Me is not worthy of Me" (Matthew 10:37; NKJV).

There is also biblical instruction to parents to "train up a child in the way he should go . . ."(Proverbs 22:6; NKJV). In New Testament teaching, parents have a responsibility to raise their children in a nurturing environment that will foster a love toward themselves and God: "And you, fathers, do not provoke your children to wrath, but bring them up in the training and admonition of the Lord" (Ephesians 6:4; NKJV). Children raised in abusive or godless homes must do everything they can to break curses themselves.

The nuclear family is preeminent in our biblical code of ethics. This value has profound effects on the stability of society, without which there can be no true progress. The Fifth Commandment lays the foundation for wholesome attitudes toward the family and establishes requirements for its leadership and faithfulness of its members. Proper application of it by both parents and children would cure most of the ails of society.

Horizontal Law

The next five commandments govern our horizontal relationships. How we interact with each other is of paramount importance to our God. God's code gives five simple rules upon which to build our lives, our families, and the whole fabric of our society.

6) "You shall not Murder . . ." v. 17

This command is often mistranslated "do not kill," which is not the correct usage of the original language. This injunction is to prohibit the taking of a human life such that it would constitute a capital crime—in other words, murder or reckless homicide. Since the first four commandments make clear who God is, it is also clear that only God can sanction the taking of a life; which he does—the punishment proscribed by God for a murder is capital punishment. (Genesis 9:6). Therefore, taking a life maliciously, violently, intentionally, is the supreme crime of which any man is capable and warrants the supreme punishment: the death penalty.

Taking a life maliciously, violently, intentionally, is the supreme crime of which any man is capable.

There is also strong language in the writings of Moses, that the shedding of innocent human life defiles the land in which it takes place. "Do not pollute the land where you are. Bloodshed pollutes the land, and atonement cannot be made for the land on which blood has been shed, except by the blood of the one who shed it" (Numbers 35:33). Life is in the blood, and innocent blood, shed unto the ground brings "bloodguilt" onto that place, thus this commandment is critically important in terms of the Israelites living in the Promised Land.

God spoke to Cain after he killed his brother, Abel, in the first recorded murder in the history of the human race: "The voice of your brother's blood is crying to me from the ground. And now you are cursed from the ground, which has opened its mouth to receive your brother's blood from your hand" (Genesis 4:10–11, ESV). And God further defined this great sin as a sin against Himself, declaring that as we are made in His image: "Whoever sheds the blood of man, by man shall his blood be shed, for God made man in his own image" (Genesis 9:6, ESV).

Responsibility for bloodguilt also extended in the Old Testament to areas of negligent homicide. A man who failed to build a railing around the roof of his house or provide normal and adequate safe guards against accidents would incur bloodguilt if someone fell and died. The owner of a bull that was known to have a habit of goring could be put to death if he failed to keep the animal confined and the bull killed a man or woman. The Torah also instructs that homicidal animals were also to be stoned to death and the carcass burned.

As with all of these commandments, one of the consequences was that since no one is exempt from this law, it elevates the value of all human life. It is just as wrong for a prince to kill a pauper as a pauper a prince. With one stroke of His finger God made all men, everywhere, equal in this respect.

7) "You shall not commit adultery . . ." v. 18

This command is pretty straightforward. There is to be no sexual intercourse between a man and a woman when one or the other is married but not to each other. Thus, God is sanctifying the institution of marriage in a special way. And one can wisely extrapolate that all sex outside of the sanctity of marriage is sin because, regardless of when or if one marries, sex before that marriage will be with someone who is likely headed to a marriage and, in God's eyes, is already promised in purity to that person.

Stop and think about this: Even if you are engaged to be married, God has established as a foundational law for society that there is to be no sex outside of marriage. Intending to get married, even shortly after the sex, does not sanctify it in the eyes of God. The wedding vows are directed toward three parties: yourself (I promise to keep myself pure in this relationship); your spouse (I am promising you I will keep myself pure in this relationship); and God (I declare You are Lord of my marriage and Judge over my promises). It is through these promises with God and the community as witnesses that a covenant relationship is established, anointed, and sanctified. A marriage bed faithful to these vows is undefiled and honorable (Hebrews 13:4). Jesus went on to say that to indulge thoughts about sex outside of marriage was against the law. The word used is to hold lust-filled "thoughts" in your mind. James says that lust . . . "when it is conceived" . . . gives birth to sin (James 1:15; KJV).

So here is the deal: God sanctifies the institution of marriage. It is the foundation of our civilization. The nuclear family—man, woman, children—is the means by which humanity is propagated, and it is the trust and unity within families that holds society together like the bricks that form a great tabernacle. Every social study regarding every conceivable subject shows the children of stable marriages to be better off than divorced, or single-parent homes.

> God sanctifies the institution of marriage. It is the foundation of our civilization.

Adultery was identified as a capital crime in Leviticus and Deuteronomy. However, Jesus showed mercy and no condemnation for a woman apparently caught in adultery (John 8:3–11). The context shows that Jesus was wise to the accusers' hidden motives against Him. So He used the incident to reveal *their* sin and reveal what the true, fulfilled purpose of the seemingly harsh law is.

Adultery destroys families. The capital punishment prescribed for it established the depth of the crime and the value of what it destroys. Without rejecting the legitimacy of the sanction, Jesus nevertheless demonstrated His mission to fulfill the true heart of the law by applying it to restore instead of just to punish. He set the adulteress free from her guilt and admonished her to sin no more. The fulfilled law of love and redemption in Christ means that adultery, as destructive to lives as it can be, is *not* an unpardonable sin. And through the redemptive power of Christ, homes damaged by it can be restored. God can and will forgive. God can and will bring healing to broken homes and to persons raised in broken homes. God can and will bring peace and reconciliation to the repentant.

Jesus changed and sharpened our understanding of the purpose of justice. But He didn't devalue the guiltiness of law-breakers whom He seeks to restore. Adultery will always be a capital crime because it destroys the most valuable things in creation—human lives. The capital punishment for it in the Old Testament was a needed lesson to mankind to affirm this unchangeable value. But that is only the first proposition. Jesus shows us the second and most revealing proposition—though sinners are guilty and deserve judgment, He came so that what is lost may be restored.

8) "You shall not steal . . ." v. 19

This command is viewed by some Jewish scholars to mean, "do not kidnap," a capital crime, since it is grouped with murder and adultery. Also, thievery and a variety of situational punishments are detailed elsewhere in the law and are clearly distinguished from kidnapping. The vast majority of scholars agree, however, that the Eighth Commandment means exactly what it says: It is sin to take what is not yours. And it applies to all men everywhere, including governments, regardless of circumstances.

> The eighth commandment means exactly what it says: It is sin to take what is not yours.

The concept of property rights is more of a western idea but it owes its origin to the Eighth Commandment. What is mine is mine, and no one has any right under any circumstances to steal it from me. But the importance of the commandment goes beyond just protection of my property rights. The fact is, everything ultimately belongs to God. If God has given you custody of something, then for me to steal it is the same as saying it doesn't belong to God; it belongs to me. This is just as blasphemous as Lucifer's sin of presuming to usurp God's rightful glory when he proposed to raise his throne above that of God (Isaiah 14:12–14).

Theft for any reason is wrong. If you find something that is not yours, the rightful owner needs to be found if at all possible. In Jewish tradition it is even taught that it is theft to waste a shopkeeper's time with questions and demonstrations of a product when you already know you are going to purchase elsewhere, such as on-line. It's called the Shopkeeper's Law, and the American Retail Association estimates that losses from this particular type of theft measures in the billions.

The obvious but unspoken implication of the eighth Commandment is that the appropriate, God-ordained way to acquire what we want is to do so lawfully and morally—by working for it (Proverbs 12:11, 14, 14:23, 21:25, 28:19; 2 Thessalonians 3:10). The Bible also mandates, however, that we strive to protect the innocent and provide for those incapable of taking care of themselves so they will not be tempted to steal. The Apostle James says that true religion is this: "to look after orphans and widows in their distress . . ." (James 1:27).

9) "You shall not give false testimony against your neighbor. . . ." v. 20

In a way, bearing false witness about someone is theft in that it is stealing the truth and replacing it with a lie. However, lying in this way is far worse than stealing because the direct objective is to harm another individual. Typically, one lies to cover up one's guilt and escape the consequences. Lying to *shift* guilt to another, perhaps innocent, person compounds the liar's sin with new victims. It is a mockery of God and a blatant denial that He is the Lord of Truth. Lying is not just wrong because it hurts people and tears away at everything that is good, as with all sin it is a blasphemous disregard of who God is, pure and simple.

> Bearing false witness about someone is theft in that it is stealing the truth and replacing it with a lie.

Today, the most common way we all disregard this injunction is to engage in gossip. We all do it but that certainly doesn't make it right. So often when we engage in gossip we don't have the facts and yet we pass on hearsay, usually with negative connotation, as if we know the facts and are a witness to them. The Apostle Paul was not kind towards people who engage in such activity: "And besides they learn to *be* idle, wandering about from house to house, and not only idle but also gossips and busybodies, saying things which they ought not" (1 Timothy 5:13; NKJV). Solomon says in Proverbs 26:28: "A lying tongue hates *those who are* crushed by it . . ." Do we "hate" people? Passing on negative, harmful, hurtful statements is hateful and God is NOT pleased.

10) "You shall not covet your neighbor's wife . . . house . . . land . . . anything . . ." v. 21

The Horizontal Law deals with what some call the predatory sins. And the Tenth Commandment deals with the great sin that many wise teachers say is at the heart of all predatory sin. Coveting involves self-worship because it single-mindedly focuses on what self wants and justifies obsessing about it. We are forbidden by God to desire and to plan how we may obtain that which God has given to another. This commandment, as do the others, upholds that God is our source. He is the source of our life, wife, and supply. Everything God gives honor us. Resentment that God hasn't given me something He has given to another is covetousness, especially if I then lust for that person's blessing. If we expect respect from others for how God has blessed us, we can understand and respect this for others. Coveting another person's stuff shows a fundamental lack of understanding about Kingdom living. Failure in this truth will lead to failure in the Promised Land.

Bottom Line

So there you have them: The greatest equalizing social force known to man and the foundation for our code of ethics, our law, and our morality as they were handed directly from the One True God to man. They truly are the basics of life. If we give a central place to these fundamental laws in our regular devotions, we will grow in our understanding of their central place in our lives in the Promised Land. How much better off would we be if we could go back to that time in our history when we collectively believed that?

My subtitle, "We've got to get back to the basics of life," is from the Willie Nelson/Waylon Jennings song "Luckenbach, Texas." One of the stanzas says:

So baby, let's sell your diamond ring
Buy some boots and faded jeans and go away
This coat and tie is choking me
In your high society you cry all day
We've been so busy keepin' up with the Jones
Four car garage and we're still building on
Maybe it's time we got back to the basics of love[8]

As you can see, I got the line wrong. It's not "get back to the basics of *life*" it's "get back to the basics of *love*." And isn't that what the Ten Commandments really are—a code of ethics lovingly given to us by our Creator for our better good? If we as individuals and as a society would get our priorities straight and understood these commandments for what they are and from Whom they come, we could all get back to the basics of love.

After pondering this chapter for some time, however, I have come, to a more powerful conclusion. My favorite Bible for daily devotion is the *NIV Chronological Bible,* edited by F. Lagard Smith. In it, all the books of the Bible are arranged according to when biblical events occurred and duplicated events are harmonized and presented together. It is a very easy and enjoyable version of the Bible to use.

It occurs to me that the very first entry into our modern Bible was literally written by God, and it was these Ten Commandments. These were God's Words literally hand written by God onto the living rock of Mount Sinai. God Himself was the first scribe of His own Word. Moses collected the tablets, and during the decades that followed he penned, as God's second scribe, the first five books of the Old Testament. But the astonishing point is that God's Word was officially initiated by His own hand in direct contradiction to any of the false precepts of higher criticism that seek to relegate God's Word to mere human imaginations.

Think about that and let the truth of it sink in. God Himself, personally, distilled into ten simple statements—some believe into ten simple declarative words—the instructions for human kind to form a productive society with reverence to Him as its focal point. Though the history of Western civilization is marred by the failings of human kind to live precisely by these commands, we can readily see the progress made by their adherents versus they that deny them. There really are skyscrapers in New York and there really are suicide bombers in the Middle East.

Consider then the profound affect adhering to the Ten Commandments would make in our individual lives and those of others dear to us. Talk about getting more promise out of your land . . . WOW!

PRINCIPLE #4
ONE PLACE OF WORSHIP

Church—You Got to Go and You Got to Stay

———

*These are the decrees and laws you must be careful to follow in the
land that the LORD, the God of your ancestors, has given you to
possess—as long as you live in the land. Destroy completely all the
places on the high mountains, on the hills and under every spreading
tree, where the nations you are dispossessing worship their gods.
Break down their altars, smash their sacred stones and burn their
Asherah poles in the fire; cute down the idols of their gods and wipe
out their names from those places. You must not worship the
LORD your God in their way.*

DEUTERONOMY 12:1–4

———

It is a reoccurring theme in Deuteronomy that God has given the Promised Land to the children of Israel in order to have a people in the earth and in that place that would have a proper understanding of Him and relate to Him properly. In so doing, He fully intended that they displace and dispossess the pagan people there and with them their detestable religious practices. To our modern sensibilities, telling the Jews to kill everybody and everything in the Land doesn't seem to be a very tolerant solution to the problem, and it isn't. Lest you feel sorry for the Canaanites, realize that for forty years they had heard the stories of God's wonders for Israel, His deliverance of them from bondage and Egypt's destruction, the Red Sea crossing, the column of smoke and fire, and forty years of miraculous provision. No doubt the Canaanites sent spies of their own over the years. And Joshua reveals the Canaanites knew Israel was coming to claim the land.

But in defiance, they remained in their cities absorbed in their unspeakable perversions and horrible sacrificial practices. There was plenty of time for them to leave. Even at Jericho, God instructed Israel to march around the city for seven days before sounding the trumpets. Jericho had every reason to know it was doomed and had a week to depart. Canaan was the focus of an ancient oral tradition and was long known (though disregarded) as promised to certain of Abraham's descendants.

That all of Jericho knew what they faced and how they could escape is evidenced by the prostitute Rahab, who spoke to Israel's spies about the common knowledge of God's miracles for them. Rahab was among the lowest of Jericho's people, yet her act of courage and faith in helping the spies escape brought her deliverance and acceptance within Israel, and it left the prideful hold-outs of Jericho with no excuses or access to mercy. One wonders what glories might have come out of Jericho if it's leaders had humbly lead their people out to greet Israel and dedicate their city to the purposes of Abraham's God. Indeed, Rehab was not only accepted into the ranks of Israel, but she also was in the line that eventually produced King David and Jesus Himself.

But that command from God—to destroy the evil in Canaan—is for us today a metaphorical, but no less commanding, truth. We are a pluralistic society and I do not believe God would have us behave in a prejudicial or condemning manner toward anybody for any reason . . . ever. I do believe, however, these passages teach that neither are we to compromise on God's Law or be ashamed of our belief in the Lord Jesus Christ. We need not modify our proper worship of God or standards of morality for any reason, or anybody . . . ever!

> We must never compromise our faith in the Lord Jesus Christ.

The first four verses of Deuteronomy 12 emphasize the importance of what God shares in the following verses, which present to us one of most crucial principles for getting more promise out of our land.

You must not worship the LORD your God in their way. But you are to seek the place the LORD your God will choose from among all your tribes to put his Name there for his dwelling. To that place you must go; there bring your burnt offerings and sacrifices, your tithes and special gifts, what you have vowed to give and your freewill offerings, and the firstborn of your herds and flocks. There, in the presence of the LORD your God, you and your families shall eat and shall rejoice in everything you have put your hand to, because the LORD your God has blessed you.

DEUTERONOMY 12:4–7

". . . seek the place the LORD your God will choose . . . to put his Name . . ." (v. 5) There, you bring your tithes and offerings. There, you have fellowship with believers of like precious faith. There, you corporately worship God. Church! You got to go to Church.

> Church! You got to go to Church.

We are specifically told to *not* worship God in the manner of the world, but we are to worship Him in a place: a place of worship. I believe in a Bible-believing, Christ-centered, salvation-teaching, Holy Spirit-led, God-praising, breaking-bread-together, New Testament Church. To such a place every believer is called to make a home, to serve faithfully, and to grow with; and to such a place we must go if we want to get more promise out of our land. God continues speaking in Deuteronomy:

You are not to do as we do here today, everyone doing as they see fit, since you have not yet reached the resting place and the inheritance the LORD your God is giving you. But you will cross the Jordan and settle in the land the LORD your God is giving you as an inheritance, and he will give you rest from all your enemies around you so that you will live in safety. Then to the place the LORD your God will choose as a dwelling for his Name—there you are to bring everything I command you: your burnt offerings and sacrifices, your tithes and special gifts, and all the choice possessions you have vowed to the LORD. And there rejoice before the LORD your God—you, your sons and daughters, your male and female servants, and the Levites from your towns who have no allotment or inheritance of their own. Be careful not to sacrifice your burnt offerings anywhere you please. Offer them only at the place the LORD will choose in one of your tribes, and there observe everything I command you.

DEUTERONOMY 12:8–14

From these scriptures, I see three principles for New Testament believers to embrace in order to see their Christian walk improved and experience all the promise that this "Land" holds for us:

1) Regular church attendance is vital to all aspects of your life.
2) God will lead you to the right church for you.
3) Church-hopping is unscriptural and detrimental to your growth; therefore commit to active membership of the church you are led to.

Church—You Got to Go and You Got to Stay

"All Christian people ought to go to church each and every week, unless hindered by sickness, or necessary work, or some other necessity" (*Haley's Bible Handbook*).[2] The author of the Book of Hebrews puts it more eloquently:

Let us hold unswervingly to the hope we profess, for he who promised is faithful. And let us consider how we may spur one another on toward love and good deeds, not giving up meeting together, as some are in the habit of doing, but encouraging one another—and all the more as you see the Day approaching.

HEBREWS 10:23–25

The strong message is clear: There is no replacement for vital involvement in a nurturing church community. Let's break down and examine this scripture more closely.

"Let us hold unswervingly to the hope we profess . . ." (v. 23) I know you have hopes and dreams or you wouldn't still be reading this book. You hope for a better life, to be a better Christian, to see your children better cared for. You have hopes for a better marriage, for a deeper relationship with God, and hopes to mature spiritually. We all have hopes like these and many more.

"And let us consider how . . ." (v. 24) How do we get that something those hopes? How do we move from a place of hoping for something to experiencing it? What can we do if all our efforts thus far have fallen short?

Wouldn't it be great if we could get help and find support—if we could be around other people who could be a good influence in our lives and the lives of our children? People who could "spur us on toward love and good deeds"?

Staying home to watch sports or hanging out at Starbucks hasn't done much. Sleeping in and relaxing around the house all Sunday is nice but such a dead end. Reading novels entertains and the news informs but neither will transform me. Going to the movies or the lake or the game are all fun, and even good things in their place, but I don't think any of them will answer my greatest needs.

". . . [Let us not give up] meeting together, as some are in the habit of doing . . ." (v. 25) What can I do to obtain the hopes that I have? What to do . . . What to do? I know!!! Let's go to church!!! Let's do what the Bible tells us to do! The world and all of its restaurants, movies, and sporting events will not spur you on toward love and good deeds. Those are not the places where you can encourage one another. You've got to go to church!

The Church's One Foundation

Jesus says in Matthew 16:18: "And I tell you that you are Peter, and on this rock I will build my church, and the gates of Hades will not overcome it."

Jesus did not mean that Peter was the rock. He meant that the truth Peter had boldly spoken from God about who Jesus is would be the foundation rock upon which His church would be built. The Church is the body of Christ. We, His disciples, who comprise the universal Church of Christ, are His body on earth in this day and hour. Appointing a place where His body can gather and worship corporately is a concept as old as the earliest hope for the Promised Land. Even Jesus taught and worshipped primarily in synagogues throughout Israel and sometimes in the Temple in Jerusalem.

The church was founded by Jesus and He is the heart of the church. The church exists to bear witness to Christ. People's lives are literally changed by the Good News of Jesus Christ. So it is the mission of the church to exalt Christ, so that He may do His work in the hearts and minds of people.

The Conduit of God's Blessing

> Going to church is an act of worship . . . a spiritual discipline. But it's also a privilege that yields blessings.

Going to church is an act of worship. We should do it as an act of faith and not convenience. And as such, it is a spiritual discipline. But it is also a privilege that yields great blessings, for the individual and for families, that can't be had any other way. Fellowship and service with fellow believers are irresistibly life changing. Our Lord has established His church to be a conduit of blessing to His people and, through them, to bring His life and blessing to the world. If all Christians would come to church routinely our churches would overflow, our tithe baskets would be full, and our ability to reach the world for Christ would be complete.

So then faith comes by hearing, and hearing by the word of God.

ROMANS 10:17; NKJV

Where else but church are you going to go to hear the Word of God preached? Praise God those who genuinely can't get to a church can join a service and hear the Word on television or via the Internet. For the rest of us, what excuse do we have? Further, do you know what businesses pay for the kind of teaching you will receive at the right church? I have paid speakers $5,000–10,000 to speak at company meetings. Some were technical in nature but most were positive, motivational speakers designed to help my employees be more productive by being more excited about being productive.

The Word of God isn't just about moral law and spiritual growth. The wisdom in God's Word will change your life! You can't get this kind of teaching anywhere else in the world. You need to be in a church that is immersed in God's Word. You'll find it filled with words of life and power. God's words of power and life help me understand the issues that affect my life. They teach me how to cope and overcome challenges and disappointments. And most importantly, they teach me who I am in Christ. Powerful preaching helps my faith, increases my understanding of scripture, and emboldens me to make changes in my life.

Fashionable Excuses

You shall utterly destroy all the places where the nations which you shall dispossess served their gods, on the high mountains and on the hills and under every green tree. And you shall destroy their altars, break their sacred pillars, and burn their wooden images with fire; you shall cut down the carved images of their gods and destroy their names from that place. You shall not worship the LORD your God with such things.

DEUTERONOMY 12:2–4; NKJV; EMPHASIS ADDED

There are many excuses offered for not going to church. I am sure you have heard it said: "Well, I love God but I just don't like being around church people." "I don't have to go to church to worship God, I can just go sit under a tree and meditate on Him." "I like to go fishing and I can just appreciate nature and all that out there on my boat." "I don't have to go to church to be a Christian." "I do not want to hang out with a bunch of judgmental, religious nuts, etc., etc."

> When it comes to God, you don't get to make the rules!

There is only one little problem: When it comes to God, you don't get to make the rules! God doesn't suggest, He *declares* how He is to be worshipped. And He declares that His people shall come together and confess Him publically. It's very convenient for those who shy from such a commitment to believe they can worship God by just appreciating nature. Nature is God's handiwork and we do love and appreciate it, but "You shall not worship the LORD your God with such things." Nature is not a sanctuary set apart by God for His worship. Nature is good and beautiful, albeit corrupted by the fall, but it is not *sacred* or *set apart* as a holy place or sanctuary. The local church sanctuary is the proper place set apart for the worship of our Lord as His people.

So Much for Excuses

I am never convinced by excuses. People are not really worshipping God in any of these replacement activities. They are not reading their Bible and openly confessing it as truth or confessing Christ and His finished work. The only part of His creation they are worshipping is themselves as they exalt their will above God's will that He has plainly declared: "You shall not worship the LORD your God with such things" (Deuteronomy 12:4; NKJV).

As for not liking church people, how can we fairly reject people we don't even know? Of course hypocrites can be found in church—about as frequently as they're found anywhere else. Hypocrisy is a human character flaw, not a design flaw of God's church. Church is exactly where flawed people need to be. Do you know anyone who isn't in need of change in their lives or improvement in their character? The answer to that is obvious if Jesus is the comparison. All of us are sinners in need of grace, unconditional acceptance, conviction of sin, spiritual leadership, and every good gift God pours through a church where Christ is lifted up and His people are challenged to put Him first in their lives. Let's be honest:

> Church is exactly where flawed people need to be.

Offensive people don't keep us from our work or our extended families within which we all have members that annoy us at times. Applying a different standard to church is itself hypocritical. We need the care of God's appointed place of worship at least as much as we need our jobs. We work to support our lives. But functioning as people of God, growing in His grace, is first and foremost what we are created to live *for*.

Of course, going to church doesn't make one a Christian! The point is that close, transparent connection with other Christians in a church makes one a *growing* Christian. And if one isn't growing, he is soon decaying. We are like water. If we aren't flowing, we'll soon be stagnating.

"Hey, I don't have to go to church to show God I love Him." Oh, really! Even though God commands it in both Testaments (Leviticus 23:3; Hebrews 10:24–25)? How loving does it seem to disobey a loving God who says He has carved your name on His palm (Isaiah 49:16)? Just to be flippant I sometimes say, "Can you really be a good drunk and never go to a bar?" How can we say we love God and yet lack the commitment or desire to go to His house of worship? And yet people do. So often these same people who say they love God substitute church attendance with trivial recreational activities. What a slap in the face that must be to Jesus who literally died for them! God forgive me for every time I was cavalier in my attitude about worshipping Him in a corporate meeting of His people in His house.

You say you can't find a church you like? Ask, seek, and knock on God's door (Matthew 7:7–11). If you are willing for your heart to be totally His, He will lead you to where He wants you. And it may not be where you would first choose.

There you shall take your burnt offerings, your sacrifices, your tithes, the heave offerings of your hand, your vowed offerings, your freewill offerings, and the firstborn of your herds and flocks. And there you shall eat before the LORD your God, and you shall rejoice in all to which you have put your hand, you and your households, in which the LORD your God has blessed you.

DEUTERONOMY 12:6–7; NKJV

Notice the presumption of blessings upon those who do what God says. "There" you will take your offerings and "there" you will celebrate those blessings, acknowledging God as your source and supply. It is "there you shall eat before the Lord." This corresponds to Communion for the New Testament believer. It is "there" you are called to worship the Lord through your tithing, which acknowledges that God owns it all. It is "there" you will present the "heave offerings of your hand," which are your voluntary gifts into God's work out of gratitude for His blessing. It is "there" God has made a place of worship for you.

> Notice the presumption of blessings upon those who do what God says.

Same Name, New Place

Moses continues in Deuteronomy where he makes clear this principle of Promised Land living:

You shall not at all do as we are doing here today—every man doing whatever is right in his own eyes—for as yet you have not come to the rest and the inheritance which the LORD your God is giving you. But when you cross over the Jordan and dwell in the land which the LORD your God is giving you to inherit, and He gives you rest from all your enemies round about, so that you dwell in safety, then there will be the place where the LORD your God chooses to make His name abide."

DEUTERONOMY 12:8–11; NKJV

Moses clearly states that the way the Israelites were worshipping God would change after they entered the Promised Land. In the wilderness, they were nomadic with no particular place set apart as their home and certainly no fixed place for their sanctuary of worship. God revealed through Moses that in the Promised Land His presence would no longer be in the pillar of smoke and fire. God was going to appoint a place where His name would abide. In other words, Israel would have a fixed place where they could know God was with them—a place where His name would be known and proclaimed—a sanctified (set apart) place where His glory would dwell. This place would become the central place of worship for Israel.

Since God's dealings with Israel are a metaphor for us, I believe God will choose the place of worship for each of us too. God will speak to you and you will feel called to the right church for you. And will know it when you find it. "There you shall bring all mand you" (v. 11).

There will be a particular place, a particular church where God will place His name for you. You will know it because He will give you peace about making it your church home. This will be the church you are supposed to be a part of, where you are to put down your roots.

And as you put down healthy roots, your spiritual strength will grow like both an oak and a willow tree. As an oak tree, you are so deeply rooted that no ill wind of adversity can blow you away. As a willow tree, you can sway and give without breaking as the Lord brings fresh winds of direction to you and your church from time to time.

And you shall rejoice before the LORD your God, you and your sons and your daughters, your male and female servants . . .

DEUTERONOMY 12:12; NKJV

God is saying: *There in that place of worship where my Name abides is where you bring your first fruits as I bring increase into your life.* This is God's command. It is not of men. There you are to rejoice before the Lord. And notice it is not a solitary calling. The Word indicates we are to bring our families, and I take it that we should urge our employees, co-workers, and friends to enter in as well. One of the core social values of both the Old and New Testaments is hospitality for strangers. We should be seeking them out also to be welcomed and nurtured.

Church-Hopping

Take heed to yourself that you do not offer your burnt offerings in
every place that you see . . .

DEUTERONOMY 12:13; NKJV

The message seems clear if we read this scripture with our New Testament eyes: We are called to have a church home. Church-hopping is detrimental to this calling. It is seldom about diligent seeking within a reasonable goal of finding a church home. Church-hopping is usually done to ease the conscience about church-going while avoiding the personal cost of commitment to one. God's stated will is that we endeavor to find *the* church where He has placed His name for us and make its people our people, warts and all.

If God has called you to a place, do not let a man run you off; nor follow a man to another church if God hasn't called you there. If you are drawn to a church by the notoriety of the minister or some of its celebrated members, or by anything to do with man, then your core motives for finding a church would seem to be man-centered. If you want to find the right church you must desire, above all other concerns, to be led to the church where God has placed His name for you.

There will always be reasons at every church to be upset. People will always find a way to disappoint you. *The grass is always greener on the other side of the fence* applies to churches as well. We, however, are called to a church by God for God's purposes. So before
e churches, make sure God is calling you to do so. Talk
or, especially if you are upset. God is not cavalier. Once

He leads you to a church home, He is unlikely to uproot you without strong confirmation. Stick with your church home and let it become part of you. Make friends there, volunteer there, and serve there. Show yourself faithful to the body of Christ that meets there. Make it *your* church, not just the pastor's church! Grow a sense of responsibility over it. Bring your tithes and offerings there. Tell your friends about your church and invite people. As your commitment grows, so will your love and enthusiasm (Luke 12:34).

The Bottom Line

One of the essential misunderstandings we have as a society is that we want the blessing so we can be faithful. Often the attitude is that if God would bless me then I would be faithful, because as things stand I can't afford to be faithful. It's as if our unfaithfulness is God's fault. But God doesn't work that way at all. God is looking for the faithful person He can bless.

Jesus teaches us that greater opportunity for blessings follow our faithfulness in small things. Faithfulness in church attendance may seem like a small thing. I can't tell you how many Bible-believing Christians I know who love God, are born again, pray regularly, post wonderful scriptures on Facebook . . . but can't get themselves to church once a week for a one-hour-and-fifteen-minute service!! Who do we think God is? And what do we think is the nominal level of faithfulness we ought to display toward the Host of Heaven? What smaller thing can we find to do faithfully than find a church where we can regularly be fed the wisdom of God and grow a family of friends who stick closer than brothers? I don't see the downside here. Heaven help our hard hearts if we can't focus our time and attention on our Heavenly Father by coming to church.

It is God's instruction that we worship Him *His* way and not *our* way—at *His* place of choosing, not *our* place of choosing, and in obedience to all *He* has commanded. He promises that we will be blessed mightily if we heed Him in this principle of the Promised Land.

PRINCIPLE #5 TITHING

You Got to Give . . . Whether You Get or Not . . . But You Will!

Honor the LORD with your wealth, with the firstfruits of all your crops; then your barns will be filled to overflowing, and your vats will brim over with new wine.

PROVERBS 3:9–10

When you have entered the land the LORD your God is giving you as an inheritance and have taken possession of it and settled in it, take some of the firstfruits of all that you produce from the soil of the land the LORD your God is giving you and put them in a basket. Then go to the place the LORD your God will choose as a dwelling for his Name and say to the priest in office at the time, "I declare today to the LORD your God that I have come to the land the LORD swore to our ancestors to give us." The priest shall take the basket from your hands and set it down in front of the altar of the LORD your God.

DEUTERONOMY 26:1–4

In everything I did, I showed you that by this kind of hard work we must help the weak, remembering the words the Lord Jesus himself said: 'It is more blessed to give than to receive.'

ACTS 20:35

———

Today's Christian can readily understand the simple mercy of giving to those in need, but may find it difficult to understand the Old Testament teachings about things like the tithe, first-fruits, alms, wave offerings, fellowship offerings, and alter gifts. Without a doubt, the Old Testament regulations on giving are very complex. The Bible, however, teaches in both Testaments that believers are required to be givers through both acts of mercy and through regular offerings to the Lord. Furthermore, throughout the Bible one thing is abundantly clear: There is a blessing on giving! You can't out-give God. It sounds simple, but so many Christians today fail to let this core truth sink in and set them free to enter and prosper in the Promised Land.

> Throughout the Bible one thing is abundantly clear: There is a blessing on giving! You can't out-give God.

There are over 130 verses in the

ig us to give and show mercy out of our resources. If
iving at will is so heavily emphasized in scripture, how

126

much more serious should we be about God's direct commands about giving back to Him as well?

The above passages from Proverbs 3 and Deuteronomy 26 each have an underlying understanding that have to do with a particular type of giving that God commands. Our faithfulness in tithing (or giving 10% of your income to God through your church) probably more than in any other spiritual discipline, reveals the true picture of how we see God. And how we see God affects our view of everything else. Giving generously does reveal a generous nature; but tithing to God's house, as we'll see, is a command that challenges our wills and our perceptions about who owns our treasure.

The presumption in the above verses is that God is responsible for all our prosperity. We have God to thank and acknowledge for all the good fruit of our lives and livelihoods. Clearly, God is the ultimate owner of all creation and all that arises out of it. So it is reasonable for God to instruct that we acknowledge Him as our source and the true owner of everything we have by tithing with a grateful heart. That's all, and it's not much considering all the promises God attaches to our faithfulness in tithing.

When we return to God the first 10% of any increase He has given us, we are, above all, expressing worship of Him as the Lord of the increase. When we are slack or rebellious in worshipping God this way, we are essentially testifying that we are the real lord of our treasure and productivity and that God's Lordship is merely symbolic or liturgical. I like the saying, *God is Lord of all or He is no lord at all.*

No, if the Bible is clear about anything, it is clear that God is Lord of Creation and all its fullness—that means everything that comes out of creation. Worshipping God as Lord of all we are and all we have by tithing to Him as He blesses us is a biblical imperative given in both the Old and New Testaments. And surely obedience to God is its own blessing, but worshipping Him with our tithes involves a special promise of blessing from Him. In fact, God even dares us to test Him in this, as we'll see.

There are two passages regarding tithing in the book of Deuteronomy. A detailed study of these passages would reveal a complex system of giving that we can better understand in three general forms:

1. Worship (giving to the Temple and the priesthood);
2. Sacrifice (burnt offerings on the alter directly to God); and
3. Support (gifts to priests and alms to the poor).

It is important to understand that each was separate and distinct from the other. Technically, the "first-fruits" mentioned in Proverbs 3 and Deuteronomy 26 are also a specific kind of worship offering that is a little different in practice from the tithe, but the meaning is the same. God gives the land, the seed, the herds, and even the strength of our hands. Israel was to say amen to this truth by giving back to Him the first gatherings of fruit. The point here is *first* fruits. The first-fruits of the harvest season were wholly devoted to God because in the biblical worldview, first things represent the whole. The first-born of each family, human, and animal was to be consecrated to God (Exodus 13:1–2). The first city God gave into the hands of Israel, Jericho, was to be consecrated to God and nothing was to be taken as personal spoils (Joshua 6:17–18). The first or central tree of the Garden of Eden was devoted to God and its fruit was not to be eaten. First-things from God are to be recognized as "devoted things" (v. 18) to God. If you would be perfect in your tithing worship of God and make an active recognition that He is the source of the whole, the best way would be to devote to God not 10% of your earnings but the *first* 10%. Treat it as belonging to God and just as consecrated to God as the city of Jericho or the Tree of the Knowledge of Good and Evil.

It is believed by some teachers that, as a *devoted thing* (or *haram* in Hebrew), the tithe is *destined for destruction* (the literal meaning of *haram*) if not freely offered back to God in obedience. This was the fate of Jericho since the inhabitants failed to surrender the first city willingly to God. The implication from this teaching is that an un-surrendered tithe is lost one way or another anyway. You may have a flat tire or an air conditioner compressor go out or some other untimely loss.

My guess is that when unexpected events bleed you of money that should have been a tithe, in God's economy that money can still end up, in the course of an unseen chain of events, exactly where God would have used it originally. Remember, your tithe is devoted to God. He can put it somewhere whether you want to give it or not. In other words, the tithe is only lost to the unfaithful, not to God. Everything already belongs to God and, in His sovereign control of history and

> Your tithe is devoted to God. He can put it somewhere whether you want to give it or not.

even the tiniest of things, He can move money anywhere He wants it. But what He desires is that we, His people, be His agents of ministry, mercy, and change in the world. He wants us to tithe faithfully and give generously so we will be operating within His economy and His plans, and so He can bless us accordingly.

The Tithe in God's Eyes

Bring the whole tithe into the storehouse, that there may be food in my house. Test me in this," says the LORD Almighty, "and see if I will not throw open the floodgates of heaven and pour out so much blessing that there will not be room enough to store it. I will prevent pests from devouring your crops, and the vines in your fields will not drop their fruit before it is ripe," says the LORD Almighty. "Then all the nations will call you blessed, for yours will be a delightful land," says the LORD Almighty.

MALACHI 3:10–12

In the farming economy of ancient Israel, the tithe was set apart out of each harvest for support of the Levites and the Temple. So obviously part of God's view of the tithe was as a means of support for the Temple and the spiritual servants of His people, the Levites, who had no inheritance in the Promised Land and thus no means to produce for their own needs.

As touched on earlier, throughout the Bible there is continually seen a basic spiritual principle: There is a blessing attached to giving. And though the tithe from our perspective is an act of worship we owe God, from God's perspective it appears to be the same as anything else He desires to respond to with blessing when we are faithful to His commands. Malachi 3 tells us God undoubtedly will bless those who tithe. The promise of blessing is pretty all-encompassing. What more could we ask in exchange for a token contribution to God's work? If we meditate long and hard on this promise and take it seriously we should come to see the trade off just that way.

But for many folks, especially during economic hard times, forfeiting 10% may not be such a token thing. For many, it may be the difference between paying rent or not. God understands this hard choice better than we do. But think of it this way: The tithe is the only choice He addresses in His Word where He invites us—He implores us to test Him. "Test Me," says the Lord God; in effect, "Let Me show Myself strong on your behalf. Let Me pour out blessings from heaven upon you and prove why your dwelling place with Me is called the Promised Land."

God could have merely commanded that we bring a tithe of all into His house of worship. But instead, He commits Himself to respond to the tither. God puts Himself, the truth of His Word, and all that He represents on trial. God put the basis of your faith in Him on trial: *Tithe and see if I will not open the windows of heaven and pour out a blessing such that you cannot contain it all* (Malachi 3:10; paraphrased).

Incredibly, God challenges the believer's complete confidence in Him and hinges the veracity of scripture on the principle of tithing!

Where Do You Bring Your Tithe?

The priest shall take the basket from your hands and set it down in front of the altar of the LORD your God. Then you shall declare before the LORD your God: "My father was a wandering Aramean, and he went down into Egypt with a few people and lived there and became a great nation, powerful and numerous. But the Egyptians mistreated us and made us suffer, subjecting us to harsh labor. Then we cried out to the LORD, the God of our ancestors, and the LORD heard our voice and saw our misery, toil and oppression. So the LORD brought us out of Egypt with a mighty hand and an outstretched arm, with great terror and with signs and wonders. He brought us to this place and gave us this land, a land flowing with milk and honey; and now I bring the firstfruits of the soil that you, LORD, have given me." Place the basket before the LORD your God and bow down before him. Then you and the Levites and the foreigners residing among you shall rejoice in all the good things the LORD your God has given to you and your household.

DEUTERONOMY 26:4–11

The first part of this scripture portion supports what we'll uncover below about the local church being the place where you are to bring your tithe—the alter of the Lord; that place where the Lord has placed His name for you and guided you to bring your worship of Him and service to His people.

But what I want you to see first is how, in verses 5–10, the confession of the worshipper puts the whole issue of giving to God in clear perspective. This confession could be a figurative confession for believers today. As we've already seen, Israel's experience is a picture of our experience of redemption in Christ. Egypt is a type and shadow of the world system within which we strive to live

Christian lives. As unbelievers, we lived supporting that system as slaves to the temporary satisfaction of sin and selfish interests. But it's degrading, and, thankfully, many escape the abuse of addiction to this system through a saving knowledge of the Lord Jesus. At some point, we each cried out to the Lord and the Lord heard our voices and saw our misery and oppression. And with every challenge to our faith in the face of every enemy of our souls, the Lord will bring us out of *Egypt* with a mighty hand and an outstretched arm, with miraculous signs and wonders. The parallels are perfect because the same mighty and loving God is the promise keeper for both ancient Israel and the church of Jesus Christ.

That puts it all into perspective. How little even the greatest among us can do to appropriately respond to what God has done and is doing for us. All we can do is worship Him! It starts with bringing to Him the best of what we are and the best of what we have. We don't even have to guess about what pleases Him as worshippers of other gods must do. Our God tells us to bring to Him the sacred portion of that which He has given us in the first place—the first portion that names it as God's provision—the tithe. It acknowledges our Savior as the giver of our new life. It is to celebrate our freedom from the world. It is to acknowledge God as our source and supply. It is to say amen to the truth and principles of kingdom living in God's Word.

> Our God tells us to bring to Him the sacred portion of that which He has given us.

I Have Not Eaten Any of the Sacred Portion

*When you have finished setting aside a tenth of all your produce in
the third year, the year of the tithe, you shall give it to the Levite,
the foreigner, the fatherless and the widow, so that they may eat
in your towns and be satisfied. Then say to the LORD your God:
"I have removed from my house the sacred portion and have
given it to the Levite, the foreigner, the fatherless and the widow,
according to all you commanded. I have not turned aside from your
commands nor have I forgotten any of them. I have not eaten any
of the sacred portion while I was in mourning, nor have I removed
any of it while I was unclean, nor have I offered any of it to the
dead. I have obeyed the LORD my God; I have done everything
you commanded me.*

DEUTERONOMY 26:12–14

I like the term *Sacred Portion*. It is sacred because it has no other
purpose but to do the work of the Lord as directed by Him. The
tithe is set apart to give to your church. This is a sacred work that
the passage also indicates is to be systematic, regular, and routine in
its stewardship of the finances the Lord provides.

The principle Moses is delivering to Israel shows we are to do
more than tithe to our church. Israel was to bring alms and gifts
over and above the first tithe to provide for the full-time servants of
God and for others in need. For Israel this was systematized in a separate and additional tithe set apart every third year. There was yet
another tithe meant to pay for personal pilgrimages to the Temple,
but we needn't explore that since the purpose again was to worship

and serve God. The point we can take from Moses is that with our tithes the church itself should be active in supporting missionaries, mercy ministries, and anyone in the body (or a stranger) who is in great need. I believe that the Church should then "tithe" to missions, missionaries, and benevolent donations. (My own church devotes 10% of its collections to these works outside the church.) But each believer, after giving his tithe to the church, should also be ready to give to others in need. Why? Because the church, and believers specifically, are agents of God's mercy. We love because He first loved us (1 John 4:19).

Most commonly in ancient times the greatest needs were felt by widows and orphans, which is why they receive special attention in the passage. There were no civic or government services for them and there were few careers available to women, which is why so many women in desperation turned to prostitution. It is the duty of God's people to answer with their generosity to prevent such injustice and tragedy. We should be ready to respond when the Holy Spirit prompts us to answer a need.

"Giving to the dead" (Deuteronomy 26:14) is analogous to using the sacred potion for a night out on the town, buying a new outfit, or spending it selfishly any other way. Again, it is sacred because it is set apart to serve God's purposes and show His name great. Even giving your tithe to the homeless guy on the corner is not appropriate, as he will most likely spend it on the dead. Giving your tithe to your

> Your first and only recipient of your tithe is your church.

friend or family member is obviously not the equivalent of giving it to the Lord. Your first and only recipient of your tithe is your church, where you worship the Lord your God. After giving to the church, then you may and should prayerfully give over and above the tithe to the needy as directed by the Holy Spirit, or perhaps to special ministry efforts within your church.

The Four Truths of Giving to God

Tithing becomes an expression of our knowledge of and faith in the Almighty. It is our acknowledgment that without God we would not have what we have, be who we are, nor enjoy where we are in life. So to cap off this chapter I'll present four general truths regarding the tithe that we must embrace to get more promise out of the Promised Land.

1. There is no greater evidence of Who you perceive God to be and of your faith in Him than the importance you place on giving to His church.

This is true on so many levels. Do you believe in God? Do you believe the members of your church are God's people? If you resist giving to your church, perhaps your belief is weak. The Bible says that where your money is there your heart is also (Matthew 6:21; Luke 12:34). It also says you cannot serve both God and money (Matthew 6:24; Luke 16:13)! Look at your checkbook and you will better see where your heart is. Are your tithes to your church evidence of your faith in Him? Or does your checkbook reveal that your god is your stomach (Philippians 3:19)? Upon whom do you depend for your blessings in life, Jesus Christ or J.C. Penney?

Your faithfulness in this area is a litmus test for what you truly believe. If you were absolutely convinced above all things that there is a God and he is a rewarder of those who diligently seek Him (Hebrews 11:6), you would *run* to your church to give your tithes and offerings. The Lord loves a cheerful giver (2 Corinthians 9:7). I submit to you that all faith-filled givers are indeed cheerful when giving. And why not? First, you are getting to worship your Eternal Creator knowing He actually sees you doing it. Second, what you are actually doing is giving thanks for His blessings in your life as if God didn't already deserve the highest worship just for who He is. And third, He has promised to give it back anyway "pressed down, shaken together, and running over" (Luke 6:38). Hallelujah! Where's my checkbook?

2. There are eternal consequences regarding your practice of giving. We can begin to understand this from Jesus' parable of the "Rich Fool."

And he told them this parable: "The ground of a certain rich man yielded an abundant harvest. He thought to himself, 'What shall I do? I have no place to store my crops.' "Then he said, 'This is what I'll do. I will tear down my barns and build bigger ones, and there I will store my surplus grain. And I'll say to myself, "You have plenty of grain laid up for many years. Take life easy; eat, drink and be merry."' "But God said to him, 'You fool! This very night your life will be demanded from you. Then who will get what you have prepared for yourself?' "This is how it will be with whoever stores up things for themselves but is not rich toward God."

LUKE 12:16–21

Jesus' parable tells us that our attitude and use of our resources has eternal consequences. As Christians, our goals are to hear God say to us: "Well done, my good and faithful servant," not: "You fool!"

> Our goals are to hear, "Well done, my good and faithful servant."

Perhaps you get a big promotion, a raise, income tax return, or a surprise refund of some sort. Is your first reaction to go and buy that *thing* you have been wanting? Or is your first reaction to honor God and thank Him for the gifts of life you enjoy?

It seems clear Jesus isn't teaching that God dislikes us having things. The man in the parable was already rich. Being rich wasn't what earned his rebuke from God. What earned the rebuke was that his things had him. His attitude was: How can I hoard more and protect it all for my own use and satisfy all my own desires? The rich man saw his wealth as the only god he needed.

Suppose I were to set up a table in any downtown area and give out $100 bills to people walking past with the sole condition being that they give me a $10 bill in exchange. How many would take me up on that deal? Would you? That, in a nutshell, is tithing. So, if you have complete faith in God, you believe to your core that He is your source and supply, and you understand that being a faithful steward of His blessings has eternal consequences, it is easy to give back to Him. In fact, giving becomes a privilege and a cheerful act of worship.

If, on the other hand, you say you can't tithe, doesn't that really say that you do not believe that God is your source and your supply? Or that you do not trust Him and His promises in this area?

3. Tithing is an act of worship.

When you tithe, remember you are returning to God what is already His. It is an act of worshipful obedience prayerfully, reverently, and cheerfully placed on the alter with an attitude of thanksgiving for God's faithfulness to give increase. Your church and your pastor are responsible to God for the wise administration of the tithe. While, sadly, sometimes men fail in their responsibilities, your tithe given in faith to God will not fail. Your hands are clean, and your gift "will not return to you void" (Isaiah 55:11). This is more of God's economy at work. He is in control of all resources so ultimately it doesn't matter what men do.

As an act of pure worship, your tithe should be offered without condition or direction. It is to be a pure act of acknowledging God's *worth*, which is the origin of the old English word *worship* or *worthship*. Occasionally, you may feel led to give gifts for specific purposes, which is wonderful and will carry the same

> As an act of pure worship, your tithe should be offered without condition or direction.

promise of blessing from God as the tithe. But such gifts should not be substituted for the tithe. The tithe is a Holy thing, a devoted thing, God's sanctified portion that is set apart before it is even given by the worshipper.

Related to that, we need to recognize that our service to the church is not a worthy substitute for our tithe. Reasoning of this nature displays a begrudging attitude: "I am doing 'X' for God so I shouldn't have to tithe." It laughably implies that tithing, in addition to service, would put God in debt. It does not display cheerful giving. Even if one could rationalize that donated time and talents are equivalent to financial support, the fact remains that it is bartering with God. It is not worshipping Him. There are exchange transactions between us and God, mostly having to do with our great needs and His abundant grace. The tithe, however, is not a commodity for trade. It is our debt to God from the moment of our birth and a privileged one at that. The problem with thinking service is a replacement for tithing is a lack of understanding about what tithing means and what we are commanded to tithe out of.

Our commitments of service are, of course, valuable acts of love for God's people and high worship we offer our King. But they are not the same as tithing our material increase. In the verses about tithing we've studied, the focus is upon tithing out of what is produced from the land. This naturally correlates to agriculture being the prominent livelihood for the children of Israel. We can assume, though, this doesn't mean fishermen, tradesmen, and merchants were off the hook. God is merciful to give increase to everyone who labors. In good conscience, we tithe whatever form of increase God gives to testify that He is the originator of all resources and their increase. So it's reasonable to say, if prosperity affords us an increase of disposable time, we should view it as an increase of blessing from God and acknowledge that by opening our hearts to greater service to His people. In effect, your time of service is a tithe of the time resource God has given you. The same principle was in effect for the Sabbath Law, which was to acknowledge that God is the giver of all our days. You alone, though, must decide if your service is in proportion to how God has blessed you with spare time.

But I do not believe you can reason that: "I give ALL my free time to the church, so surely that means I don't have to tithe too?" Again, you are bartering with God. Right, wrong, or indifferent, God made no such allowance in His Word for bartering with Him.

4. The tithe is to be an act of sacrifice.
Some people have it in their minds that tithing, specifically giving 10% of our income, is not a New Testament principle; and that even in the Old Testament it was an incredibly complex system of taxation for a theocratic form of government. As such, they say, "We New Testament believers need not look to these Old Testament principles for guidance, but specifically only give as we are able—cheerfully, of course." I suppose that translates to *nothing* if you can't be cheerful in the process or if you determine you just aren't able to give.

The book of Malachi is the last book in the Old Testament. In Texas, we tend to believe last words are true words—that they are important words. It stands to reason that we would all want our own last words to be our most important. The book of Malachi was written as God's last words to the children of Israel. It's the last book of the Old Testament and most scholars agree it was the latest book in the canon to be written. Malachi 3:10, in which we are instructed to tithe, is merely fourteen verses from Matthew 1:1— literally, one page of my Bible separates the two.

God had given His chosen people His law so they would be blessed. He gave them the Promised Land so they would be blessed. He wrote them love songs (the Psalms) and books of wisdom (Proverbs–Ecclesiastics) so they would be blessed. He sent fiery prophets to admonish and guide them so they would be blessed. In a single last effort, He sent Malachi to give a final word so they would be blessed.

The book of Malachi completed the Old Testament. It is sacred scripture. Jesus read from it, He taught it, He preached it, and He fulfilled it. Malachi tells us, in the context of tithing, to worship God with acceptable sacrifices.

> *"A son honors his father, and a slave his master. If I am a father, where is the honor due me? If I am a master, where is the respect due me?" says the LORD Almighty. "It is you priests who show contempt for my name.*
>
> *"But you ask, 'How have we shown contempt for your name?'*
>
> *"By offering defiled food on my altar.*
>
> *"But you ask, 'How have we defiled you?'*

"By saying that the LORD's table is contemptible. When you bring blind animals for sacrifice, is that not wrong? When you sacrifice lame or diseased animals, is that not wrong? Try offering them to your governor! Would he be pleased with you? Would he accept you?" says the LORD Almighty.

MALACHI 1:6–8

We dishonor God when we bring a *lame* gift to our King. Isn't that how you feel when you get a lame gift at Christmas time from your boss or company? After all you have done for them all year, and they give you a personalized coffee mug engraved with the company logo—and not even your name. *How lame*, you think. And that is exactly what we do when, instead of bringing the tithe, we tip God with a five as the plate goes by. That is the equivalent of what some in Old Testament times did by bringing their unmarketable animals to the alter instead of sacrificing something choice and irreplaceable, the way God Himself deserves to been seen. See the point? God is rightfully insulted when we approach Him as an afterthought or an inconvenient obligation—someone we need to appease like a neighbor's dog, so we throw Him a bone with a little meat on it. We give Him something we won't miss. God expresses His grief at this:

> How lame. . . . when instead of bringing the tithe we tip God with a five.

Oh, that one of you would shut the temple doors, so that you would not light useless fires on my altar! I am not pleased with you," says the LORD Almighty, "and I will accept no offering from your hands. My name will be great among the nations, from where the sun rises to where it sets. In every place incense and pure offerings will be brought to me, because my name will be great among the nations," says the LORD Almighty.

MALACHI 1:10–11

God is seeking to make His name great on the earth. He begins by making His name great in churches that teach this message. But He would just as soon shut the doors of the church that accepts *lame* gifts offered to Him.

"When you bring injured, lame or diseased animals and offer them as sacrifices, should I accept them from your hands?" says the LORD. "Cursed is the cheat who has an acceptable male in his flock and vows to give it, but then sacrifices a blemished animal to the Lord. For I am a great king," says the LORD Almighty, "and my name is to be feared among the nations.

MALACHI 1:13

Cursed is he (God calls that person a cheat) who has the means to give sacrificially, to be a part of God's endeavor to make His name great, but fails to do so. Does that really need any further amplification? The end of the rich fool in Jesus' parable was nothing if not a curse. Malachi goes on in chapter 2:

"And now, you priests, this warning is for you. . . ." "Because of you I will rebuke your descendants; I will smear on your faces the dung from your festival sacrifices . . ." "For the lips of a priest ought to preserve knowledge, because he is the messenger of the LORD Almighty and people seek instruction from his mouth. But you have turned from the way and by your teaching have caused many to stumble . . ."

MALACHI 1:1, 3, 7–8

Here I take particular note that I, as a pastor, have a holy obligation to communicate God's truth regarding making sacrifices to Him. Otherwise, He will rub my face with dung from lame sacrifices! I'm not sure what kind of experience that would translate to from today's versions of lame sacrifices, but I don't want to find out. A sacrifice is supposed to be just that—a sacrifice! So if it doesn't feel like a sacrifice it probably isn't. That isn't to say it should fill you with dread. On the contrary, if you worship God for Who He is your sacrifice should give you great joy as only something that is a sacrifice could. The sacrificial aspect of it is what makes it a great thing. It is greatly pleasing to God and fulfilling to you.

Bottom Line

I have a clear obligation to teach that we are to give sacrificially to God. Our commitment to do so speaks to God, loud and clear, what we think of Him. I believe without a doubt that a tithe, or 10% of our income, is the scripturally-mandated amount we should give. For some, a true sacrifice may be more; but for the vast majority of us, 10% of our income represents both the tithe and a sacrifice. I, however, part company with those that contend that the blessing is *only* upon gifts given over and above the tithe. No—Malachi, it seems to me, explicitly says that if I will tithe—God will open the windows of heaven upon me (Malachi 3:10).

Often I am asked questions like: Do we tithe off the gross or the net? Or, is it really important that the first check be the tithe check? Others will say to me that they just can't comprehend that if they are giving away 10% to good causes, why that isn't the same as tithing. My answer is: Fortunately or unfortunately, we don't get to make the rules.

There are two powerful instances where Jesus personally reacted to the giving patterns of God followers. First, in Mark 12:41–43, Jesus marveled at the poor widow who gave two small copper coins and immortalized her faith and love for God as far superior to the noble religious leaders who gave modestly, most likely exactly 10% of the gross out of their abundance.

Jesus saw the same lame values as those of the religious leaders in the rich young ruler (Luke18:18) who did "everything" he needed to do to inherit eternal life. He followed the Law to the letter, including paying precise tithes. He had just one flaw. Jesus showed the young man that by not being generous with his wealth, he had failed to follow the heart of the Law. When Jesus challenged him in a way that would change his heart, he went away sorrowful, unwilling to make the sacrifice. Like the rich fool in Luke 12, his wealth was his true god. The rich young ruler was, no doubt, a tither; but that in and of itself did not reveal a selfless heart in him to Jesus.

The poor widow gave all she had; completely trusting that God would meet her need. Though it was only roughly the equivalent of two pennies, she got the attention of God (Jesus). *Hers was a demonstration of true worship.*

When we ask questions about exactly when to give, where exactly to give it, and exactly how much to give, are we trying to negotiate with God? Worse, does it say our thoughts and opinions on His Word are higher than His thoughts? And what does that say about our trust in Him?

So, to me, the answer is that for the vast majority of us who have to manage our money in order to not run out every month, 10% of the gross usually represents a sacrifice. It is the scripturally supported, sacred potion we can lovingly place at the feet of our Lord, which He will, in turn, lovingly bless. Further, it should be the first use of our income. If we are tithing off the net because we are trying to 'split hairs' with God or because we begrudge giving Him the larger amount, our "blessing" will be equally small if there is any blessing at all. It is hard for God to bless a hard heart. Also, all biblical examples of tithing are given to the priest in the Temple or to the Lord through the administration of His church—period.

> Ten percent of the gross usually represents a sacrifice. It is the scripturally supported, sacred potion we can lovingly place at the feet of our Lord, which He will, in turn, lovingly bless.

As God prospers our obedience to Him in this area and we give above and beyond the tithe, God will, I believe, bless such giving exponentially. If you are not a tither but you receive this message and with a sincere heart endeavor to organize your finances to be able to tithe and give sacrificially in the meantime, I can only imagine that God, who knows your heart, your true intentions, and your motivations, can and will bless such gifts given sacrificially to Him. This may seem to contradict the imperative to tithe in order to be blessed, so I would like to reiterate: God knows. We cannot kid God. God knows if you are giving to the dead. In other words, God knows if you can't *seem* to tithe, if it is because included in your necessary monthly expenses are frivolous or even unnecessary expenses. God also knows our hearts and whether He is first place in your heart or, for example, movie theaters are. So it is absolutely imperative that you continue to use any blessing to organize your finances properly to become a tither and not spend it on dead things. To put it plain and simple: You must get to the place where you are tithing above all other uses of your money, first and foremost. To get more Promise out of your Land bring the whole tithe into the place where God has placed His name for you . . . your church.

PRINCIPLE #6
CANCELING DEBTS

Forgiveness Is Next to Godliness

---

*At the end of every seven years you must cancel debts. This is how it
is to be done: Every creditor shall cancel any loan they have made to
a fellow Israelite. They shall not require payment from anyone among
their own people, because the LORD's time for canceling debts has
been proclaimed. . . . For the LORD your God will bless you as he
has promised, and you will lend to many nations but will borrow from
none. You will rule over many nations but none will rule over you.*

DEUTERONOMY 15:1–2, 6

The Year for Canceling Debts

Deuteronomy 15 has a rather amazing provision regarding Promised Land living. Every seventh year is a sabbatical year, and verse 1 says that at the end of that sabbatical year all debts must be canceled. Specifically, God's people must account fellow Hebrews free of any outstanding debts owed to them. Further, any fellow Hebrews who might have sold himself into another's service is to be released, set free, and supplied with adequate provisions to start a new life. There is an explicit promise from the Lord that in so doing, the "Lord your God will bless you in everything you do." Obviously, God is immediately answering the natural anxiety any creditor would have about losing what is owed to him. It almost sounds like another way God was setting Himself up to be tested and proven faithful.

As I read this passage in Deuteronomy, I am reminded that I am a debtor to God, due to my sins, and He has released me and blessed me to start a new life as well! How beautiful, then, does this passage become as we reflect upon what Jesus has done for us? Jesus paid the price and the interest on our debt on our behalf, so that we may be restored into our original place with God. Compare the passage in Deuteronomy to the following New Testament passages:

Luke 4:18–19 "The Spirit of the Lord is on me, because he has anointed me to proclaim good news to the poor. He has sent me to proclaim freedom for the prisoners and recovery of sight for the blind, to set the oppressed free, to proclaim the year of the Lord's favor."

Matthew 6:12 And forgive us our debts, as we also have forgiven our debtors.

The first passage is Jesus quoting Isaiah to declare Himself the fulfillment of that prophesy and a perfect fulfillment of what the Sabbath year mandate pictured—the year of the Lord's Favor. It seems clear that the Sabbath year Promised Land principle was meant not just to build the peoples' trust in God, but to prepare their minds to receive the gospel of deliverance. The second scripture from Matthew is part of His instructions to the disciples regarding how to pray—more commonly known as the Lord's Prayer. Both carry the spirit of the Law of Restitution or debt forgiveness found in the book of Deuteronomy.

As New Testament believers, we are told explicitly to live in a spirit of forgiveness continually. Matthew 6:14 says, "If you forgive men when they sin against you, your heavenly Father will forgive you. But if you do not forgive men their sins, your Father will not forgive your sins." It seems that *unconditional* grace from the Father has a condition: With the same measure that you forgive, forgiveness will be measured out to you, and you will be blessed accordingly!

Throughout the New Testament, we are instructed to live out the gospel of Jesus Christ and to not just enjoy its benefits but to

> With the same measure that you forgive, forgiveness will be measured out to you.

model its instructions to reflect the goodness we experience to those who need that goodness. Chief among our blessings is that we have been forgiven our sins against God and man. How much more, then, should we reflect that spirit of forgiveness back to those that have wronged us?

Further, this not a suggestion. Though it does carry a blessing, it is not a quid pro quo as it may appear at first glance. It is a commandment from God reaffirmed by Jesus and may be one of the hardest tests of our faith we ever face. Forgiveness is the core substance of Christianity and the true proving ground of every believer and follower of Christ. We are to forgive, set free of debt, those that have sinned against us because we have been forgiven so much. You might ask, "When is the right time to forgive? When my offender asks for it or when I'm offended?" In several passages, such as 1 Peter 1:18–20 and Revelation 13:8, it is revealed that God's purpose to forgive and redeem us was established before He even created the world. Think about that as we look further at Deuteronomy 15 with our New Testament glasses on.

Sabbath Forgiveness, New Testament Style

At the end of every seven years you must cancel debts. This is how it is to be done: Every creditor shall cancel any loan they have made to a fellow Israelite. They shall not require payment from anyone among their own people, because the LORD's time for canceling debts has been proclaimed.

DEUTERONOMY 15:1–2

We are required to cancel debts. In this regard we can view this commandment as a metaphor for our New Testament understanding that we are to "forgive those who have sinned against me, as I have been forgiven." What is involved in forgiveness, that is *real* forgiveness the way Jesus would forgive? First, it is letting the hurt go. Not expecting restitution. No eye for an eye; no tooth for a tooth— but real forgiveness. To those who maliciously hurt us, Jesus even says we are to turn the other cheek to demonstrate to our offender how far we separate them from the hurt. Then, to forgive the debt is to cancel the debt and forget about it . . . forever. God says He will not remember our forgiven offenses and He separates them from us as far as the east is from the west—an infinite distance (Hebrews 10:17; Psalm 103:12).

Have you ever lent someone money, perhaps a friend, expecting to be repaid? Then, as time passes, you realize that someone doesn't intend to repay you. And every time you see the person they act like everything is normal and the debt doesn't exist. Perhaps you've even learned your money bought some luxury or paid for a trip. You have been wronged and your friend genuinely owes you. This is the tough part: Who is being hurt as this situation continues with no change—you or your friend? The answer surprisingly is *you*. For the time being, your friend seems to have a clear conscience while you retain the feelings of hurt and betrayal. Something has to change for you to be free. If you wait for your friend to repent and repay you, or at least apologize and ask you to forgive the debt, you may be hurting for a very long time.

An injustice done is exactly the same in most instances. It is the injured party who retains the hurt in most instances and is damaged in the process. The offenders who hurt us may be oblivious to the damage done or simply uncaring about it. Their guilt is between them and God and will certainly be judged. But it is the injured party who holds a grudge that is most damaged. Someone once told me that holding a grudge is like swallowing poison and expecting the other person to die. Retaining the pain is like accepting a curse. Let it go. It is the best thing you can do for yourself, and you will experience a blessing.

Blessed or Cursed

> *And forgive us our debts, as we also have forgiven our debtors.*
> *And lead us not into temptation, but deliver us from the evil one.*
> *For if you forgive other people when they sin against you, your heavenly Father will also forgive you. But if you do not forgive others their sins, your Father will not forgive your sins.*
>
> MATTHEW 6:12–15

The New Testament requirement to forgive carries with it an explicit promise: We will be forgiven as we forgive. How wonderfully liberating forgiveness is, especially when it is we who are in the wrong! What a relief to be forgiven! No other feeling compares. It's like the purest form of love because someone has sacrificed to set you free. It is a huge weight taken off your back. It is to be re-born;

it is a fresh start, a new beginning to do things differently. How rich is the man who can forgive a wrong! What strength and determination; how lion-hearted he is! It exhibits far more strength to forgive than to carry a grudge.

And how miserable is the one who tight-fistedly holds on to wrongs? The reality is that it is the extreme of selfishness. *I have been hurt. I have the power to extend forgiveness but I will not. I have not been repaid or received an apology.* Have you known someone who cannot seem to forgive? They may be able to cover up their misery and poverty of spirit most of the time but the truth can't help but come out at times. Unforgiveness taints the victim's outlook on life. Children that cannot forgive a parent; a spouse with an unforgiven grievance; anyone who can't let go a wrong are themselves held captive by their anger. Often, they experience physical ailments, psychological stresses, and extreme unhappiness.

Anger is a negative, defeating emotion. It is no fun to be mad. It is no fun to be around an angry person—it robs you of its polar opposite: peace. It's like clutching a spiny seed pod with sharp points digging into your palm deeper and deeper as you squeeze tighter to conceal it. If you don't let it go so you can heal, eventually there will be no concealing the hurt. Your blood will run for all to see and may get on others. Your unforgiven hurts can even turn you into someone who brings only injury.

> Anger is a negative, defeating emotion.

Poverty is Poverty

If anyone is poor among your fellow Israelites in any of the towns of the land the LORD your God is giving you, do not be hardhearted or tightfisted toward them. Rather, be openhanded and freely lend them whatever they need. Be careful not to harbor this wicked thought: "The seventh year, the year for canceling debts, is near," so that you do not show ill will toward the needy among your fellow Israelites and give them nothing. They may then appeal to the LORD against you, and you will be found guilty of sin.

DEUTERONOMY 15:7–9

I have two thoughts to glean from the above verses: First, do you know anyone who is "poor" in spirit as a result of anger and unforgiveness? You might think these verses can only apply to material poverty but it doesn't matter what kind it is. The kind that results from unforgiveness is just as miserable, if not worse, than material poverty. People with miserable, poor, and darkened spirits are no fun to be around. Rather than avoid them, we need to approach them and freely share with them what we've been freely given—the liberating gospel of forgiveness. We need to encourage forgiveness first by modeling it and then by encouraging it in others.

My mother, God rest her soul, for all her wonderful qualities, was troubled throughout her life by a lack of forgiveness. First, her young brother died in an accident. Then her parents divorced (at a time when that was unusual). Her husband, my father, was unfaithful in the early years of their marriage. She developed a place of bitterness deep in her spirit that made her distrustful of people. She had no close friends that I know of. I can remember very few times when she seemed genuinely happy, and I never saw her express pure unbridled joy. I know this was all a result of a lack of forgiveness and holding on to the hurts of loss and betrayal. Once we spoke of heaven in this regard and she retorted to me, "I better get into heaven for all the hell I've had on earth." For her sake, I hope so too. But to you I say, don't count on that equation working for you. And the simplest sense of it is, why waste your life in bitterness? Let it go right now! Begin to live again.

Second thought: Please don't find yourself saying, "now is not the time," especially if your real motive is to savor your right to be angry. You may have provocation for anger but claiming a right to it may be pushing against what Jesus said is equivalent to murder (Matthew 5:21–26). Recognizing that you've been wronged isn't the issue. Withholding forgiveness out of some self-satisfying sense of justice is unjust and is itself worthy of judgment, as Jesus said. Indulging in vengeful anger for even a little while is dangerous to you. It is a wicked thought.

Another way we may be tempted to withhold forgiveness involves another wicked thought touched on in Deuteronomy 15: 9 above. We might find ourselves thinking, "I can't forgive that debt, the rent is coming due." Shall we wait to practice forgiveness until it is easy? How very small our faith in God's promises is proven to be with such a thought!

> Shall we wait to practice forgiveness until it is easy?

I know persistent anger and a demand for justice can feel right, and it can be virtually impossible to not feel pain from an offense for a while. Still, the truth is simple and plainly given: We are to forgive at the appointed time. When is that? Now! Do not allow the enemy of your soul time to root anger and resentment inside you. Don't let circumstances steal your joy. Give forgiveness now—ASAP—cancel that debt and restore the lost relationship. God requires this of His people, *and* you will be blessed by it.

Forgiving in Faith

Have you ever been wronged or hurt by someone? I have too. When I need to forgive, and especially when it's hard, I try to practice what I call forgiveness by faith. I go to the Lord with a simple, humble prayer in my heart. I get quiet and find it in my heart to say honestly to Him: "Lord, I am hurt and I am angry, but mostly I am embarrassed and distraught. Lord, you are going to have to help me forgive. In faith, I express forgiveness toward that person . . . now, Lord, please help to manifest that forgiveness from the inside out." I keep that prayer in my heart and seek to walk in that faith by speaking forgiveness and acting out forgiveness. Soon, I find God faithful and I am able to practice and even feel forgiveness for the one who wronged me. I challenge you to do this also with expectant faith in God's power to change your heart. In time, you will discover that you have forgiven your offender.

Forgive and *What*?

If any of your people—Hebrew men or women—sell themselves to you
and serve you six years, in the seventh year you must let them go
free. And when you release them, do not send them away empty-
handed. *Supply them liberally from your flock, your threshing floor*
and your winepress. Give to them as the LORD your God has blessed
you. Remember that you were slaves in Egypt and the LORD your
God redeemed you. That is why I give you this command today.

DEUTERONOMY 15:12–15; EMPHASIS ADDED

Again, the moral basis of God's social directive emphasized above
can be broadly applied to principles of Kingdom living. And this
may be the very hardest part: If you think forgiveness is hard, how
about forgetting the offense ever happened? ". . . when you release
them, do not send them away empty handed. . . ." In other words,
bless them and restore them just as God has forgiven you and forgotten your sins separating them from you "as far as the east is from
the west." He has thrown your offenses into the "deepest part of the
sea," never to be retrieved. Treat those you've forgiven as though
they never sinned and restore them. For a malicious offender, that
may mean offering the other cheek in some way. You are showing
that you hold them blameless and so another offense is no consequence to you. What does that have to do with restoring? Everything, because nothing is lost in the first place. Turning the other
cheek isn't about courageous defiance, as some presume. It is showing your offender that he is not making himself your enemy. For

the merely thoughtless offender, however, forgetting and restoring usually means just recapturing the lost relationship and interacting with them as though there is no offense.

Bottom Line

Of course this is hard. Frankly, it's humanly impossible. Our Father forgives perfectly while we forgive imperfectly. Your divorce has been unbearably hard, unfair; and your spouse has been unforgivably difficult. That boss was so wrong and abusive. Your partner stole from you and left you struggling. Someone has really, deeply hurt you. Only Jesus could do what I'm suggesting. But here is the most important and life-changing truth to understand about the Grace of Christ: The more of His Spirit you have controlling yours, the more He can work His miracles through you. Giving forgiveness His way is a true miracle.

> The more of His Spirit you have controlling yours the more He can work His miracles through you.

I am not advocating that you write a check to the thief who stole from you—but don't let him steal your joy too. Forgive him, release him, restore him, and preserve your dignity. If children are involved, work with your ex-spouse persistently and patiently. Don't make children choose sides. Do the right thing; in other words, the God thing and forgive all debts.

Every one of us has sinned and fallen short of the glory of God. It is only because He chose to die for us that we have any hope for eternity at all. If God so loved the world that He gave his Son for us, how dare we not forgive likewise?

One last thought: I almost don't want to mention it but it's right there in the Bible:

> *If your enemy is hungry, give him food to eat;*
> *if he is thirsty, give him water to drink.*
> *In doing this, you will heap burning coals on his head,*
> *and the LORD will reward you.*

PROVERBS 25:21–22

This sounds like a rather odd way to get revenge. Of course, revenge is no motive for a believer who is resting in God's faithfulness. But the prescription offered for offense is to return good for evil to the person who has wronged you. The best way to respond to a hurt is to do something beautiful; to be positive, respectful, and even encouraging. Even the most hard-hearted person will be struck by your dignity, peace, courage, and self-discipline. More importantly, so will the Creator of the Universe. Responding this way could be life-changing for that person and perhaps the very reason God allowed the offense.

My mother always told me that *cleanliness was next to Godliness*. The truth is that *forgiveness is next to Godliness*! And it's a surefire way to get more Promise out of your Land.

PRINCIPLE #7
FORBIDDEN FOODS

You Got to At Least Try to Be Healthy!

———

You are the children of the LORD your God. Do not cut yourselves or shave the front of your heads for the dead, for you are a people holy to the LORD your God. Out of all the peoples on the face of the earth, the LORD has chosen you to be his treasured possession.

DEUTERONOMY 14:1–2

———

Just as I began working on this chapter, Gene Simmons of KISS fame was being interviewed on television with Shannon Tweed, his only long-term partner. In spite of the fact that Simmons obnoxiously admits to thousands of sexual partners over the years, during the interview the couple quipped, "Happily unmarried for twentyt-six years." The interviewer, a young entertainment show talking-head, laughed and made light of the comment, saying we all should try living like that way. Clearly, the way of the world is not how we as God's children should live. As Christians, we know and understand that. I doubt there is anyone calling Christ Lord who believes we should forgo lawful marriage before God. A Christian couple living together as one-flesh without lawful recognition over the relationship by God and the state is clearly outside of God's will and damaging to any kind of God-blessed and fruit-filled life.

The passage in Deuteronomy 14 is simply saying that ungodly people have ungodly ways. We will not obtain God's favor by engaging or indulging in the natural habits and gratifications of those who don't know and follow God. Now, if we can believe this in the obvious issues of morality, can we apply this to practical life-style matters as well? Moses does just that in the verse immediately following the scripture above: "Do not eat any detestable thing" (v. 3). A natural reaction to that statement is to wonder what it has to do with obtaining the abundance of Christ-centered, Promised Land living.

Clean and Unclean

Moses immediately continues, in chapter 14, with a list of regulations that have become synonymous with the Jewish, or *kosher*, diet. They were wisely established by God for the health and well-being of Israel, and they were honored by Jesus during His walk on this earth. The question is, do they have any significance for us today?

Unfortunately, the average Protestant would casually dismiss and categorize these dietary guidelines as arcane, Old Testament religious observances imposed on the Jews that have no relevance to our freedom in Christ. The assumption is that pork and certain other meats, for instance, were forbidden merely to symbolize the distinction between God's people and gentiles. The resurrected Jesus did, after all, reveal to Peter in a dream about unclean animals that He had made clean what was once called unclean. And clearly the Lord was awakening Peter to the reality that the gospel was salvation to all peoples of the world and not just for the Children of Israel. This has commonly been carried further to include a formal inclusion of any and all meat as suitable for human consumption.

I find this ironic and contradictory. We view Moses' dietary principles as mere symbolic observances but Peter's dream as both symbolic and practical. I am proposing that the opposite is true. First, I believe the context of Acts shows the Lord was specifically and singularly giving Peter a spiritual truth and not in addition the termination of God's dietary principles. *Secondly, I believe God gave Moses a wise set of dietary rules that, if practiced, would benefit the physical health of His people. But God was also speaking spiritual truths through these laws that would help Israel learn who they were as a people set apart for Him.* I like to summarize the diet restrictions in this catchy way: God's principle is that you not eat anything that would eat you. I'll have more on that in a moment.

> God's principle is that you not eat anything that would eat you. I'll have more on that in a moment.

We are looking to get all the promise out of the Promised Land (our kingdom lives) it has to afford, correct? I do not know a single person who does not hold dear the promise of good health. Nor do I know a single person who could not benefit from a healthier life-style. I will go a step further and say that an enormous percentage of God-fearing Christians are overweight, out of shape, and chronically ill due to excessive, undisciplined, and irresponsible dietary habits and sedentary lifestyles. So many of us judge self-indulgent people like Gene Simmons, while indulging our own appetites with "freedom in Christ" and wondering why God is allowing our allergies, degenerative diseases, and early death. I'm not saying that all sickness and early death are always our own fault. The world we live in is, after all, a sick and dying place. Things happen and God has His invisible ways and His plans for our lives. But God also has promises that we can count on to protect and enrich us if we also live by His wisdom.

I see so many people pray for healing over conditions and diseases they probably wouldn't be suffering if they just exercised regularly and made wiser and more disciplined choices about what and how they eat and drink. I am not going to say God does not hear those prayers nor respond to them, but let me relate a story.

One day, I was working alongside an employee in one of my former businesses, and after a while she asked to take a smoke break. Stepping outside the building with her I asked, "Aren't you a little concerned about getting cancer?" She responded, "Oh no." "Why not?" "Because I pray a prayer every time I light up that I will not get cancer!" I was incredulous. "M . . . ., you can't think God answers such prayers. That would be like playing Russian roulette with a revolver and praying that God will prevent the firing pin from striking the one cylinder that contains the bullet!" I believe her self-indulgence and self-justification for smoking, in that moment, was just that presumptuous.

If you want to get all the Promise out of your Land, including enjoying a life free of diseases, YOU HAVE TO AT LEAST *TRY* TO BE HEALTHY!

I was raised with the idea that physical activity was just about work or recreation. There was never a mention of its health benefits. My father's favorite form of recreation was playing poker—not fishing or hunting, no baseball-tossing—just poker. We had a standing poker game at our house every Friday night and most Saturdays. I began to play poker as soon as I could hold cards. As a result, I never played any sports growing up. The first time I played baseball, it was for my own company's tournament team and they had to let me play. So I never got any real exercise except the little I got playing in my high school marching band, which I was allowed to substitute for PE.

I began to exercise regularly for the first time in my late thirties, mostly because I heard a preacher say we should set an example for those we love. That really cut into me because certain persons who were important to me were beginning to have serious weight problems. So right then, I decided I would begin setting a good example.

The first time I tried to run, I made it about twenty yards and got a stitch in my side so badly I nearly doubled over in pain. It seemed to take forever but my run gradually grew from a hundred yards to a mile, then two, then three, and I kept adding distance. I never ran a marathon, but I grew to love just getting out for a good long run.

> The joy of good health far out-weighs the work to obtain it!

When I was approaching fifty years of age, I joined a gym and committed to be in the best shape of my life on my fiftieth birthday. I succeeded. Now, at fifty-eight, I have excellent muscle tone and enjoy virtually ideal weight. I love to go on long bicycle rides today with my beautiful wife. The joy of good health far out-weighs the work to obtain it!

Americans are plagued with a variety of illnesses due to being overweight and out of shape. Diabetes, high blood pressure, coronary heart disease, some cancers, joint pain, on and on are brought on, or at least aggravated, by unhealthy eating—including over-eating and lack of exercise. All of these are life-limiting and potentially life-threatening disorders. Chronic illness brought on by unhealthy lifestyle is completely inconsistent with the kind of Promised Land life God intends for his children. God's prohibition against certain foods in Deuteronomy should be viewed by New Testament believers as at least a metaphor, if not a literal prescription, for God's people at all times to lead healthy lifestyles.

Don't Eat Anything That Would Eat You

I'd like to challenge you to turn to Deuteronomy 14:3 in your Bible and study the list of approved and prohibited foods for yourself.

The animals, birds, and seafood that are excluded are, for the most part, carrion eaters—meaning they will eat dead animals. Animals and birds that are approved are, for the most part, strictly herbivores. Seafood and fish that are prohibited, for the most part, live on dead or diseased organisms. The approved fish with fins and scales only eat smaller live organisms and vegetation. Essentially, God created the *dirty* animals to eat bad stuff and keep the earth clean. They were not designed with our consumption in mind.

> Dirty animals were not designed with our consumption in mind.

Lest I come across as some dietary puritan, let me confess that nobody likes a big ol' plate of bottom-dwelling, carrion-eating, deep-fat-fried catfish more than I do, along with a big side of deep fried starchy tubers (French fries) and a stack of cornmeal hush puppies deep fried in the same grease. I will also admit having strong cravings occasionally for shrimp (another bottom-dwelling carrion eater) prepared in just about any fashion. I have even been known to enjoy oysters (another carrion eater) on the half shell, which, if they aren't bad enough, are swallowed raw! With all the "detestable" meats we consume, I sometimes wonder why we don't fry up a nice plate of vulture or rat. Unlike pigs, at least rats groom themselves and find dry places to nest. I suspect we don't eat such things because we see, openly, what they dine on and are repulsed by it.

For some time, commitment to dietary health has been gaining strength in the broad Christian community, which is a good thing.

However, a parallel trend increasingly sees a vegetarian diet as the nobler and perhaps healthier choice for Christians. But it should be carefully noted that meat, per se, is not prohibited or even discouraged in the dietary law. Nor is a vegetarian diet commanded in the Bible.

Many of the approved meats listed are particularly low in fat and cholesterol while being high in protein and other nutrients. Conversely, the disapproved meats are high in cholesterol and fat, while being lower in nutrients. Some biochemists have discouraged many of the disapproved meats, especially pork, because they digest quicker and dump acids into the blood stream too quickly. The body will then take drastic measures to protect the narrow safe blood ph levels by robbing alkaline minerals from your bones and teeth, if necessary. It's no wonder that a diet heavy on pork and shellfish as well as other high acid "foods" like refined sugar and flour can result in bone and joint degeneration.[9]

What's the Beef About Meat?

As a reasonable part of a varied and healthy diet, all the "clean" meats are quite healthy and nourishing for humans. The argument is made by strict vegetarians that, unlike the smooth intestinal walls of natural carnivores such as cats and dogs, the human digestive tract isn't structured to efficiently move digested meat through it. The answer to this is that humans aren't designed to be meat eaters *exclusively*, as are cats and dogs. Obviously, an exclusively meat-based diet would be bad news for us. An expanding middle-age gut may not be mostly fat tissue but a growing storage of poorly digested, overly meat-heavy diet. Even clean meats, if not properly combined with high-fiber whole foods, will be sluggish going through your system.

We are designed by God to thrive on a broad variety of food types. Did you know that your body can begin preparing your digestive system with specific mixtures of enzymes and acids based on the mere aromas you smell as food is being prepared? This is probably why we can suddenly have an appetite when we drive through the aromas in a restaurant district. However, this doesn't mean a smorgasbord of every kind of food available is good for you. The very best diet for humans seems to be simple meals of a couple of well-paired foods and that aims for a wide variety from one meal to the next. This way, we are less likely to over-challenge our digestive systems with foods that don't combine well but we do get a broad nutrient base.

The Bible records an occasion when God Himself dined with men and approved meats were on the menu. The Angel of the Lord (God) ate beef (a choice tender calf) with Abraham who, after the meal, bargained with the Lord regarding the destruction of Sodom and Gomorrah (Genesis 18). Elijah was miraculously provided "bread and meat" by the ravens sent from God (1 Kings 17:2–6). Notice it wasn't the unclean ravens that Elijah ate, but they brought him bread and meat. Interesting that God used ceremonially unclean animals to minister to His prophet and handle his food. But the important thing is that it is evident God does not impose a vegetarian diet in Holy Scripture, and we need not hesitate to include approved meats in a balanced diet.

Balance is Key

As I said: *You have to at least try to be healthy*. But we need to also be wise when it comes to Kingdom living. That usually means remembering the principles we have been given, but also remembering the ultimate higher purpose for those principles. Paul said, because we live by the grace of God through faith, all things are permitted. But he added that not all things are *expedient* and he refused to be ruled by his appetites (1 Corinthians 6:12). We know we are no longer in debt to the Law of Moses for our right standing with God. But we also know that doesn't free us to live like the Devil, gratifying every urge our fallen souls desires.

The purpose of our salvation is to set us free from slavery to that nature in order to please God and draw all men to Christ. Those are our highest purposes in the Kingdom and of our King. So, Paul admonishes us to live above reproach and obey Christ's commands. The same ways our souls need proper nourishment for them to grow in Christ, our bodies need proper nourishment to be strong and healthy for service to Him and His people. We can't eat like pigs and then expect God to rescue us from the illnesses and weaknesses we've brought on ourselves.

> We can't eat like pigs and then expect God to rescue us from illness.

Please understand, I am not suggesting ill health from a poor diet or eating prohibited foods is sin! To the contrary, the Apostle

Paul specifically said in Colossians 2:16, "Let no man therefore judge you in meat or in drink. . . ." In 1 Timothy 4, Paul also said that God created all foods and all should be received with thanksgiving. ". . . every creature of God is good, and nothing to be refused, if it be received with thanksgiving: For it is sanctified by the word of God and prayer" (vs. 4–5; NKJV). The context seems to indicate that some unusual food has been presented and Paul is instructing the believer to accept it thankfully with prayer and not reject it. Why would Paul need to give this instruction if it weren't the normal custom of the recipient to not eat the food in question? So the issue is, why does Paul instruct liberality here? If we are to uphold the dietary principles from Moses, how do we factor in what Paul says? The answer is, again, about our higher purpose.

This relationship of Christian morality, as it affects the Christian lifestyle, was hotly debated within the Jerusalem church with Paul contending for freedom of conscience for gentile believers. Peter and the other church fathers finally conceded Paul's point and satisfied themselves with admonishing their gentile brothers to "abstain from food sacrificed to idols, from blood, from the meat of strangled animals, and from sexual immorality. You will do well to avoid these things." Notice they say that their brothers will "do well" to avoid them, not "be saved" by avoiding them.

This was a very hard thing for tough-minded Jews to come to terms with. But Paul further clarifies, in 1 Corinthians 10: what he was talking about when he deals with eating meat sacrificed to idols. On the one hand, he makes it clear that believers eat the bread of Christ and share in the atonement of His shed blood. Therefore, we must not share in the blood offered to the lies of demons (v. 18–21). Paul is clearly talking about any context involving a pagan sacrifice that then involves the believer. Eating meat sacrificed to an idol in the context of the sacrifice is the same as worshipping the idol. However, Paul then distinguishes this context with buying the same meat at the meat market or presumably receiving it at an ordinary meal. He says it's ordinary meat and to pay no mind to where it came from, not only because our conscience is clear before Christ but also because we don't want to reject the hospitality of an unbelieving host (v. 27). Paul then cautions about causing another, perhaps novice believer to stumble who may strongly object to eating the meat. In this case, Paul says to prefer the tender conscience of the believer for the time being and turn down the meat. Paul gives us the wisdom key to making sense of all this in verse 24 after restating what he said in chapter 6 about permitted but not expedient things. The one thing we must keep in mind in all choices is this:

No one should seek their own good, but the good of others.

1 Corinthians 10:24

So whether you eat or drink or whatever you do, do it all for the glory of God. Do not cause anyone to stumble, whether Jews, Greeks or the church of God—even as I try to please everyone in every way. For I am not seeking my own good but the good of many, so that they may be saved.

1 Corinthians 10:31–33

174

Our relationship with God is based solely on our relationship with Christ—not upon what we do or do not eat or drink! Paul was adamantly against continued adherence to the Jewish Law insofar as it might diminish one's reliance on the shed blood of Christ and His substitutionary death for us. We run the same risk today when we place our actions upon the alter of faith rather than our faith upon the actions of Christ. Our obedience to God's principles and our wise lifestyle choices have personal benefits as well as higher purposes. But we don't want to bring condemnation on anyone, because ultimately everything is about lifting up Christ Himself not the principles that point to Him.

> Our obedience to God's principles and our wise lifestyle choices have personal benefits as well as higher purposes.

The Bottom Line

Don't think you're off the hook. I am still saying that *you have to at least try to be healthy.* Hardly anyone I know is totally content with their weight or level of fitness. In some cases, we are literally killing ourselves with what we eat and our lack of movement. Much like Bible reading for some, we dismiss attempts to eat and exercise with: "I just can't do that," or "I'm just not an exercise person." Yet we come to God and beg His healing power after ignoring His basic precepts for our personal wellbeing. Our prayers for good health will be much more effective if they are accompanied by actions of faith. A loud and proud claim of "Praise God, by Christ's stripes I am healed!" when you are still downing a pint of ice cream every day for comfort is basically a false testimony. It's not a right-standing claim. Only the prayers and faith claims of a right-standing man avail much (James 5:16). What your right hand says, your left hand must also say. So claiming the healing power of Christ's stripes must be accompanied by proactive choices that show you mean it.

A responsible diet is the best place to start, along with some kind of exercise. Common sense and a brisk walk will suffice for most of us. The real benefit of exercise is how it saturates your tissues with oxygen. With a lack of oxygen, your cells get old and die faster than your systems can replace them. We have become so lazy and sedentary, spending countless hours per day in front of television, never breathing deeply or getting our circulation going at highway speeds.

Good health is the greatest gift one can receive. All the promises of the Promised Land pale in comparison to the promise of good health, especially when you are sick. Nothing else will as greatly detract from or add pleasure to the other promises. For that reason, I beg you—*at least try to be healthy* if you want all the Promise the Promised Land has to offer.

WHAT NOW?

The renewed man acts from new principles, by new rules,
with new ends, and in new company.

MATTHEW HENRY COMMENTARY

If you want to go swimming in the afternoon,
you got to mow yards in the morning.

DON KING

This book was written because after nearly thirty years of walking with the Lord I have observed so many Christians, including myself, hurting and not living the blessed life they believe they should be living based on what the Bible says and what they hear preached. I have heard thrilling *name it and claim it* messages on the power of faith—that God wants to bless us so He will get all the glory, and all we have to do is *believe we receive what we say.* I have been told the opposite extreme as well—that God will not answer selfish prayers only intended to change circumstances we don't like, and that true faith is about enduring and overcoming circumstances so that we become the faith-warriors for Christ that God intends us to be. I have been challenged by one person to stretch my faith by expecting a better and more productive life, and another tells me to be content with my salvation and focus on becoming like Christ. (I identify more easily with the first person's idea.) However, I do so want to be like Christ, and I know our struggles in life are meant more to make us holy than happy. But based on all of God's promises to Israel and Christ's church, I have to believe that my right-standing faith in Christ is effective for my whole life and not just my Christian character.

I also understand the role of Grace in our salvation. God reached out to us when we were in the pit, before we were church going, tithing, faith warriors who eat right. I know we do not earn our salvation, His love, or His gifts. God 'owes' no man anything. Clearly, however, He delights in the well being of His children. Scripture is clear on that point.

As I talk with some people, the blessed life always seems just beyond their reach. Why do some people seem so easily blessed while others seem to only suffer? Why can some overcome addiction, lack, or sickness while others seemingly can't?

Giving God Something to Work With

Many years ago, an evangelist came to the church I was attending. He was a very charismatic black man who came to share his testimony. I remember listening from the pews and being seized by his story. As a youth, he had become a member of a gang, much to the consternation of his Christian mother. Later, he started pimping for a lineup of prostitutes and soon became hopelessly addicted to sex, drugs, and alcohol. Before long, he committed an armed robbery of a liquor store. With increasing violence in his life, he one day got in an argument with a fellow gang member who pulled a gun and shot him. The hospital where he was taken contacted his mother, saying he was in critical condition. By the time his mother arrived, he had slipped into a coma. Just as the doctors told his mother he might not make it, his heart stopped. They told him later that his mother brushed the doctors aside, ran to his bedside, and commanded life back into his body in the name of Jesus.

That mother's bold claim of life availed more than physical life for her son. Jesus took notice of her true faith and gave her son true life. As he recovered in the hospital, he read the Bible, confessed Jesus as his savior, and even witnessed to one of his prostitutes who visited him. He left the hospital completely changed by the power of God. He never touched drugs or alcohol again. He soon married the prostitute he had led to Christ and they became prosperous evangelists to the glory of God.

I so distinctly remember sitting there in my chair and thinking, *God, what about me? Do I have to get shot and die before you will deliver me from my addictions? Come on, give me something I can use!*

It may be that you have had similar feelings. Would it surprise you to know that God is asking us the same questions? I know this because later I felt a nudge and a still small voice say to me, "Don, give me something I can use."

God may be saying to you, "Give me something I can use . . ." Give Him something He can use to bless your life. Give Him your time and attention as befitting the Creator of the Universe. Put Him first place in your Life. Put away idols in your life and realize who you are in Christ. Learn His Law and His Word, and learn to love them. Go to church, regularly and routinely. Worship Him with your tithes and offerings. Give forgiveness as you have been forgiven. Exercise discipline over your appetites. This doesn't mean make sure you always live perfectly and sinless. It means strive with a good conscience to follow Christ starting right where you are and walk in all the light and spiritual strength you have. Desire to honor Him in all your ways, hungering for more of His Spirit. Don't try to be strong against temptations or challenges. The enemy will always use your show of willpower to probe deeper into your weaknesses. Instead, try to know your Lord in the midst of challenges and He will make you strong. Get your eyes off of your problems, weaknesses, and shame and onto the One who knows you best. Give God something He can use and He will bless you! The sure Word of God promises it. I believe His promises. As far as I am concerned, that settles it.

The Promised Land is full of hills and valleys and is populated with giants. Until Christ returns, we will each be fighting giants and overcoming valleys in our lives. But the promise of the Promised

Land is also a never-ending enjoyment of milk and honey—if you live according to God's principles.

Remember the promise in Deuteronomy 15:4. In the Promised Land, there should be no poor among you. The context in which God gave that promise was material well-being, not spiritual. Often, we may be accused of taking spiritual promises and trying to make them material. In this case, God's promise is material well-being. But we can make a strong case for spiritual application as well. Live in the Promised Land God's way and not your own way and all will be well with you. God Bless you on your journey into and through the Promised Land.

ENDNOTES

1. A full translation of the mezuzah text is available at: http://www.mezuzah.net/text.html

2. Ingrid Newkirk, *The New Yorker*, April 23, 2003.

3. Peter Singer, *A New Ethic for Our Treatment of Animals*, 2nd ed. (New York: New York Review of Books, 1990), p. 19.

4. Gary Yourofsky in an interview on *The Abolitionist Online*, 2005.

5. *Radical Environmentalism*, Wikipedia, http://en.wikipedia.org/wiki/Radical_environmentalism

6. Thomas Cahill, *The Gifts of the Jews: How a Tribe of Desert Nomads Changed the Way Everyone Thinks and Feels*, Anchor Books/Nan A Talese (1999).

7. Ibid, page 142.

8. Waylon Jennings, "Luckenbach Texas," song lyrics, http://www.lyricsmania.com/luckenbach_texas_lyrics_waylon_jennings.html

9. Sellmeyer DE, Stone KL, Sebastian A, Cummings SR (January 2001). "A high ratio of dietary animal to vegetable protein increases the rate of bone loss and the risk of fracture in postmenopausal women. Study of Osteoporotic Fractures Research Group". *American Journal of Clinical Nutrition*, Vol. 73, No. 1, 118-122, January 2001. http://www.ajcn.org/content/73/1/118.full